ABUNDANT PEACE

Morihei Ueshiba, founder of Aikido, at age seventy-six.

ABUNDANT PEACE

The Biography of Morihei Ueshiba,
Founder of Aikido

JOHN STEVENS

SHAMBHALA
BOSTON & LONDON
1987

SHAMBHALA PUBLICATIONS, INC.
HORTICULTURAL HALL
300 MASSACHUSETTS AVENUE
BOSTON, MASSACHUSETTS 02115

9 8 7 6 5 4 3 2

PRINTED IN THE UNITED STATES OF AMERICA
DISTRIBUTED IN THE UNITED STATES BY RANDOM HOUSE
AND IN CANADA BY RANDOM HOUSE OF CANADA LTD.

LIBRARY OF CONGRESS CATALOGING-IN-PUBLICATION DATA
STEVENS, JOHN, 1947—
ABUNDANT PEACE.
BIBLIOGRAPHY: P.
INCLUDES INDEX.
1. UESHIBA, MORIHEI, 1883—1969.   2. MARTIAL
ARTISTS—JAPAN—BIOGRAPHY.   3. AIKIDO.   I. TITLE.
GV1113.U37S95   1987   796.8'092'4   [B]   86-29631
ISBN 0-87773-350-3 (PBK.)

PHOTOGRAPHS WERE OBTAINED FROM THE FOLLOWING SOURCES:
AIKIDO HOMBU DOJO, *AIKI NEWS*, JOHN WEATHERHILL, INC., KENSHU SUNADOMARI,
KISSHOMARU UESHIBA, MASAMITSU SUENAGA, MICHIO HIKITSUCHI,
MORIHIRO SAITO, RINJIRO SHIRATA, SADATERU ARIKAWA,
SEISEKI ABE, TAKUO TAKAOKA.

Contents

Preface

MORIHEI UESHIBA is revered throughout the world as the founder of Aikido, the most progressive and enlightened of the modern martial arts. The image of the saintly old master, barely five feet tall, effortlessly throwing a host of strapping young trainees is a familiar one. How did this little man attain such giant strength? What is the real story behind his unsurpassed martial prowess? Where do the true dimensions of his unique message lie?

While making every effort to paint an accurate portrait of the life and times of the founder of Aikido, I have focused on the why and how of Morihei's quest rather than the when and where, concentrating on a discussion of the people, events, and ideas that most influenced the master.

After prudently sifting through the huge—and frequently contradictory—written and oral literature, I have put together this biography, which I hope will both delight and stimulate the reader, as well as shed light on the essential questions "Who was Morihei Ueshiba, and what was his teaching?"

PART ONE

The Man

I am the Universe.
—MORIHEI UESHIBA

I

FOR TWO AND A HALF CENTURIES, the Tokugawa shogunate closed Japan off from the rest of the world and imposed a rigid system of controls on the citizenry. Following a series of upheavals in the nineteenth century, however, the military government tottered and then finally collapsed in 1868 when the young emperor Meiji declared the restoration of imperial rule. A fierce power struggle among various factions ensued, and it was not until 1877, upon the defeat of Takamori Saigo's diehard samurai forces, that the country was unified.

A new order, built from the ground up, was needed, and an extraordinary number of talented men and women, no longer under the oppressive thumb of the shogunate, appeared on the scene to take the challenge. A popular proverb of this period was "If the spirit is strong, there is nothing that cannot be accomplished." It was an era of innovation in all spheres of human endeavor: the old ways had to be reevaluated and renewed.

Against this exciting background of challenge, experimentation, and opportunity, Morihei Ueshiba was born on December 14, 1883.

Already parents to three daughters, Morihei's mother and father were delighted by the birth of their first (and, as it turned out, only) son, considering him a gift of the gods. A prosperous farmer and local politician, Yoroku, Morihei's powerfully built forty-year-old father, was of samurai stock; his grandfather Kichiemon was renowned for his prodigious strength and prowess in the martial arts. Morihei's mother Yuki—distantly related to the Takeda clan, custodians of a long tradition of martial arts—was a cultured woman with a deep interest in literature, art, and religion.

Morihei's birthplace, the fishing and farming village of Tanabe located in Kii (present-day Wakayama Prefecture), was in the heart of an area associated with most ancient strains of Japanese mysticism. This district, known as Kumano, was thought to be a "gateway to the Divine," and in the earliest periods of Japanese history the main shrines in the mountains there were said to be the holiest in the land—even emperors from Kyoto made pilgrimages to Kumano Shrine in order to receive its special blessings. The great mountain deity of Kumano was enshrined and worshiped in innumerable *jinja* (shrines) all over the countryside; over the centuries hundreds of saints purified themselves beneath the sacred Nachi waterfalls, home of almighty Dragon Kings; the wizard En-no-Gyoja, grand patriarch of mountain ascetics, once worked his magic nearby; and Kobo Daishi, master of Tantric Buddhism, was believed to be still alive, meditating on the "mandala peak" of Mount Koya, awaiting the dawn of a new age with the arrival of Miroku Buddha, the enlightened one of the future. Morihei was thus, from birth, immersed in an atmosphere in which the supernatural, the mysterious, and the divine were palpably present.

As a consequence of his premature birth, Morihei was rather frail and sickly as an infant. Early on, though, he displayed an insatiable interest in both esoteric and exoteric science. The boy devoured hundreds of books on all manner of subjects, being especially intrigued by mathematics and physics. Around age seven, Morihei was sent to a local temple school to study Chinese classics under the priest. Bored by the dry moralizing of the Confucian texts, Morihei implored the Shingon priest to tell him stories about Kobo Daishi's great miracles and teach him the esoteric Shingon rites, meditation techniques, and secret chants.

Shingon Buddhism employs the tantric method of realization: elaborate ritual, secret visualizations, and the rich sensual aids of art, music, and one's own body to foster enlightenment in this present existence. Specifically, Shingon makes extensive use of Sanskrit mantras and spectacular ceremonies such as the *goma* fire service. The impressionable young lad absorbed all of this sacred lore, later incorporating much of it into his mature thought.

In addition to Shingon Buddhist training, Morihei became a fervent believer in the Shinto gods of Kumano. He spent much of his free time exploring the mountain's holy sites and maintained throughout his life that guardian angels from Kumano watched over him.

Yoroku, concerned about his son's weak physique and nervous temperament, encouraged Morihei to engage in *sumo* wrestling, running, and swimming. The boy also joined the local fishing expeditions, quickly becoming adept at harpooning. Under the watchful eyes of Yoroku and a schoolteacher who took a special interest in the unusual child, Morihei gradually built up his body. Awakened to his potential power, the boy dreamed of someday turning into the strongest man in the world. He toughened his skin by dousing himself daily with ice-cold water and asking his friends to pelt him with prickly chestnuts. His power increased so much that he was called on to carry sick children on his back to the doctor in the nearest town, some fifty miles distant. The necessity of possessing adequate strength was reinforced one night when the youth witnessed his father fighting off a group of thugs sent by Yoroku's political rivals to harass him.

Morihei entered the newly opened Tanabe Middle School in 1896, at age thirteen, but left after only one year of study. He was too impatient to follow an established curriculum and disliked being confined indoors all day. Morihei subsequently enrolled in a highly regarded abacus academy. Blessed with a razor-sharp mind and a deft hand, he was acting as an assistant instructor a year later.

After graduating from the academy, Morihei took a job as an auditor at the local tax office. He performed his duties well enough to attract the offer of a transfer to the bureau in Tokyo. Morihei, never intending to be a "pencil-pusher" for the rest of his life, refused the appointment and shortly thereafter resigned his post to work on behalf of hard-pressed fishermen against the recently promulgated Fishery Industries Regulation Act. Certain wealthy operators and corrupt officials were using the law to stifle competition from poor fishermen. Indignant, the seventeen-year-old Morihei drew on his knowledge of the tax codes to defend his neighbors and also protected them against threats of violent reprisal. The final outcome of the affair is not clear, but Morihei revealed to all that he was not one to sit on the sidelines and play it safe during a controversy.

However admirable, Morihei's activism caused his councilman father no small amount of consternation. Yoroku offered Morihei a substantial financial stake, telling him to take the money and find an occupation that really suited him. Although still unsure of his calling, Morihei, ever the dreamer and dissatisfied with life in a remote village, decided to seek fame and fortune in the great metropolis of Tokyo.

Within a few months of his arrival in Tokyo at the end of 1901, Morihei was able to open a small stationery store with several employees, but his heart was not in the world of business. After falling ill with beri-beri due to a poor diet, he distributed the remaining stock to his employees, closed the store, and spent his last yen on a first-class ticket back to Tanabe, where he announced to his startled father, "Well, I left Tanabe with nothing and I returned with nothing!"

Morihei may not have been much of a merchant during his brief stay in Tokyo, but he did discover his affinity for the martial arts, greatly enjoying his study of Tenjin Shinyo Ryu *jujutsu* with a teacher called Takisaburo Tobari and his visits to a Shinkage Ryu *dojo*.

The nineteen-year-old Morihei rapidly regained his health thanks to the fresh air and wholesome food in Tanabe. In 1902 he married Hatsu Itogawa, a distant relative, and the following year was summoned to serve in Japan's armed forces.

One of the primary reasons the shogunate collapsed in 1868 was its inability to drive out the "foreign barbarians" who were demanding that Japan open its doors to Western trade. The fledgling nation was forced to negotiate a number of unequal treaties, and the new leaders, intent on avoiding colonization by Western powers, embarked on a breakneck buildup of the nation's military.

By the 1880s, the Japanese government felt strong enough to renegotiate certain treaties and, caught up in the spirit of the times, to attempt some imperialism of its own. One group favored "peaceful" expansionism through economic cooperation, while leaders of the military were, not surprisingly, bent on more coercive forms of adventurism.

When the Western powers began making inroads into China in the 1890s, Japanese militarists gained the upper hand in the government and intervened, under the pretense of liberating Korea from the yoke of Chinese oppression, on the continent in 1894. Much to the world's surprise, Japan—a virtually defenseless group of little islands in 1868—soundly defeated China in the war and dictated the terms of a highly favorable peace treaty in 1895.

Japan's emergence as Asia's premier power alarmed the Western allies; Russia, France, and Germany intimidated Japan into giving up much of the territory in Manchuria it had claimed as spoils. Although not strong enough to challenge those countries at the time, Japanese military leaders secretly vowed to avenge the humiliation. Thereafter, 55 percent of the national budget went to the armed forces. Morihei was one of thousands of recruits called up to serve in the reserves.

However, Morihei failed to meet the minimum height requirement of five feet two inches and was rejected. Bitterly disappointed, he secluded himself in the mountains, training like a madman to stretch his spine the necessary half inch, mostly by hanging from trees for hours at a time with heavy weights attached to his legs.

Much to his satisfaction, Morihei passed the physical the next year and was assigned to a regiment stationed in Osaka. Fiercely competitive and driven to compensate for his small stature, he excelled at military life. Extraordinarily fleet of foot, he was the only infantryman in the regiment who could keep up with the officers mounted on horses during the twenty-five-mile marches. Morihei was also the best at *sumo* wrestling and bayonet fighting.

Morihei used his head—literally—to make a name for himself in the army. For some years previously, he had thickened his skull by pounding it against a stone slab a hundred times each day. Officers in the old Japanese army were notorious for raining blows down upon the heads of their subordinates for the slightest infraction. More than one irascible officer fractured his knuckles on Morihei's rock-hard skull, and big bullies who picked on the diminutive soldier were knocked unconscious by a little blow. (Fifty years later during a demonstration, Morihei was struck full force on the head with a wooden sword; despite a tremendous *thunk!,* observers were astounded to hear Morihei laugh off the blow, saying, "Nothing can crack this old stone-head of mine!")

War with Russia broke out in February of 1904. Morihei was stationed in Manchuria, but the year and a half he spent there is shrouded in mystery. Despite vague references to a distinguished service record, it seems that Morihei never saw action in the conflict, reportedly because of Yoroku's secret plea to his superiors not to send the family's only son to the battlefront. (In his last years, Morihei confused his military service in China with events that occurred during the later "Mongolian Adventure.") Supposedly, Morihei's superiors urged him to make the military his career, but he declined their support and accepted his regular discharge when his regiment returned to Japan.

Following his discharge from the army, Morihei was ill and depressed. His first-hand experience with the death and destruction of war—Japan was ostensibly the victor in the conflict, which ended in September 1905, but the bitter fighting resulted in huge casualties on both sides—surely must have affected him.

During his military tour of duty, Morihei enrolled in the *dojo* of Masakatsu Nakai, an instructor of Yagyu Ryu *jujutsu,* located in Sakai. Morihei trained at the *dojo* on leave days and, after his discharge, commuted there regularly from Tanabe, eventually being rewarded with a teaching license in 1908. Additionally, Yoroku constructed a *dojo* on the family property and invited the noted teacher Kiyoichi Takagi (later ninth *dan* instructor of Kokodan *judo*) to give lessons there. Morihei trained diligently, adding to his ever-expanding knowledge of classical martial arts.

While he was making great progress with his martial arts studies and increasing his already formidable physical strength, Morihei remained in spiritual torment. He would disappear for days in the mountains, engaging in fasts and other ascetic practices, and swinging his sword for hours and hours. Every day he purified himself in ice-cold waterfalls and stormy seas. He was distant and uncommunicative to his family and friends. Something was troubling him.

Around 1909, Morihei became passionately involved in the protest movement against the government's recently enacted Shrine Consolidation Policy and came under the influence of the eccentric educator Kumakusa Minakata (1867–1941). This encounter was among the first of many "meetings with remarkable men" that Morihei had throughout his life. As a young man, Minakata had studied science in the United States, visited Cuba and the West Indies, and eventually made his way to England. There he became a professor of Japanese Studies at Cambridge and earned a reputation as an astute scientist, conducting research in various fields and making valuable contributions to the study of archaeology, anthropology, and Oriental religions. He corresponded with the Buddhist scholar D. T. Suzuki, then living in the United States, and translated several Japanese classics into English.

After eighteen years in the West, Minakata returned to Tanabe in 1904 to teach and write. Several years after his return, the government announced its Shrine Consolidation Policy. The national government had its eye on the extensive tracts owned by many local shrines and planned to merge smaller ones with bigger ones, seizing control of "excess" property for development. As a naturalist, Minakata understandably opposed this policy, which would have resulted in the destruction of wildlife sanctuaries and disrupted age-old religious traditions. Minakata organized a protest movement, enlisting the services of Morihei, among others. Morihei enthusiastically jumped on the bandwagon, making speeches, leading demonstrations, petitioning the government, and negotiating with local authorities.

Minakata, whose fiery denunciations were frequently fueled by copious amounts of rice wine, was imprisoned for several weeks following an intemperate outburst. However, with such staunch supporters as Morihei, Minakata's group prevailed and Tanabe lost very few shrines.

The dynamic Minakata—a man with an insatiable thirst for knowledge, an internationalist with vision—filled Morihei's head with the many wonders and challenges the world offered to those with the courage to seek them out.

After Morihei's first child, a daughter named Matsuko, was born in 1910, his disposition improved somewhat. He responded with enthusiasm when a friend who had visited the frontier land of Hokkaido painted a glowing picture of the opportunities that it offered; Morihei immediately arranged for an inspection tour to the distant province. After a meeting with Hokkaido's governor and a trip around the huge island, Morihei decided that the well-watered district of Shirataki in the northeast section of the island would be suitable for a permanent settlement.

Upon his return to Tanabe, Morihei arranged a recruitment meeting. Neither farming nor fishing held much promise for second and third sons in Tanabe, and a number of veterans of the Russo-Japanese War were eager to embark on a new course. All together, fifty-two families, composed of eighty-four people, signed up for the venture. Since few of the members had any savings to speak of, Morihei's father once again put up the money. On March 29, 1912, the group set out for their new homeland.

When the emigrants left Tanabe, cherry blossoms fluttered in the warm spring breeze; but when they arrived at Kitami Ridge in Hokkaido, they were greeted by a blizzard. It was not an auspicious beginning. It took the party a month to cross the treacherous ice-caked mountain pass, and not until May 20 did they reach the intended site of their new community. Shelter, of course, was the first priority, and by the time the buildings were up, it was too late to clear sufficient land to plant. They managed to cultivate the land the next year, but crops were poor, and for the initial three years everyone subsisted on potatoes, wild vegetables, and fish caught in the local rivers. As leader of the expedition, Morihei bore the brunt of the criticism dished out by the disgruntled settlers; consequently he worked without rest day and night to remedy the situation.

By 1915, the crops began giving better yields and the lumber business started turning a profit. To further promote the local economy, Morihei helped develop the area's dairy, horse-breeding, and mining industries, as well as to organize the village's health, sanitation, and educational departments. A terrible fire in 1917 that destroyed the entire village, including Morihei's home, was a severe setback; again, Morihei worked tirelessly to rebuild everything. He was elected to the village council and gained respect throughout the district as a responsible and effective leader. In fact, this period in Shirataki was the only time of Morihei's life that he behaved in a more or less conventional manner. Keenly aware that the success of the entire project largely depended on him, the usually quixotic, totally unpredictable Morihei was practical, prudent, and well organized.

During the first years at Shirataki, Morihei's martial arts training consisted mostly of wrestling with huge logs and throwing the highwaymen whom he often encountered on his solitary trips. (Although Morihei dealt harshly with common criminals and escaped convicts, he was compassionate toward runaway indentured laborers—virtual slaves, lured to Hokkaido under false pretenses—and ransomed or otherwise arranged for the release of dozens of these unfortunates.) Morihei was also skilled at subduing rampaging Hokkaido bears. He calmly shared his mountain hut and food with the huge beasts, and it is said that the bears would see him off down the mountain when he returned to the village.

In the Hokkaido period, Morihei was obsessed with physical power and endurance. He single-handedly felled five hundred trees a year, uprooted stumps with his bare hands, broke thick branches across his back, and played tug-of-war with draft horses. He performed his meditations outdoors and continued the daily practice of dousing himself with ice-cold water, even in the midst of the frigid Hokkaido winters; Morihei taught himself to generate internal heat, similar to that of Tibetan "sky-clad" hermits. He told his disciples that the spot where he purified himself in the river did not freeze over even in the coldest part of the year!

On a lighter note, Morihei, for the first and apparently only time in his otherwise rigidly upright life, had a sweetheart, a young girl from Tanabe who took tender care of the gruff leader in the early Hokkaido days. The love affair came to an abrupt end with the arrival of his wife, who had been left behind in Wakayama until proper accommodations were built in Shirataki.

The most momentous event of Morihei's sojourn in Hokkaido was his meeting with Sokaku Takeda, the dreaded master of Daito Ryu Aikijutsu.

Sokaku Takeda, the last of the old-time warriors, was born in 1860 in Aizu (present-day Fukushima Prefecture). In a country of fierce samurai, Aizu warriors were among the most feared. The entire province was a "treasury of the martial arts"; training halls, offering instruction in every martial art imaginable, filled Aizu.

As soon as Sokaku could walk, the boy was taught swordsmanship, spear fighting, combat *jujutsu*, and *sumo* wrestling by his exceedingly severe grandfather Soemon and his father, Sokichi—they singed Sokaku's fingers if he failed to learn a technique quickly enough. Fortunately, the child proved to be a prodigy who cared for nothing but the martial arts.

At the age of thirteen Sokaku was apprenticed to Toma Shibuya to learn Ono Itto Ryu swordsmanship; he received that school's teaching license four years later. According to the official Daito Ryu account, Sokaku then became a live-in disciple of the celebrated Jikishinkage Ryu master Kenkichi Sakakibara; however, there is no record of Sokaku's presence in that *ryu*'s annals, and since Sokaku spoke disparagingly of Sakakibara later, it is difficult to ascertain the extent, if any, of Sokaku's training under Sakakibara. Supposedly, Sakakibara sent Sokaku to study with Shunzo Momonoi, headmaster of the Kyoshinmei Ryu, in Osaka; but, here again, Sokaku later boasted of defeating Momonoi "two out of three times."

During his teens, it appears that Sokaku actually drifted from training hall to training hall making mischief rather than studying exclusively with one master. In 1875, Sokaku's older brother suddenly died, and the young swordsman was summoned back to Aizu to assume the hereditary position of Shinto priest. Sokaku was sent to learn the basics from the distinguished scholar–martial artist–priest Saigo Tanomo, who also happened to be the last man capable of teaching the secret *oshiki-uchi* techniques of the Takeda clan.

Tanomo, chief adviser to the Aizu lords, was one of the few retainers to urge the Aizu leaders not to resist the new Meiji government. Tanomo was overruled, unfortunately, and hundreds of his compatriots perished in furious but ultimately futile rebellion against the imperial forces in 1868. During the final assault, Tanomo was dispatched to Hakodate in Hokkaido to organize a last-ditch defense by the country's remaining loyalists to the Tokugawa regime. Meanwhile, the imperial forces overwhelmed the Aizu defenders; as the enemy approached their compound, Tanomo's mother, his wife, his four daughters, and fourteen other members of the household committed suicide en masse to avoid the disgrace of being taken prisoner. It is said that when an aide of Tanomo's arrived at the scene, he found one of the daughters still alive. "Friend or foe?" she whispered. Upon hearing the reply "Friend!" the young girl calmly requested that the soldier finish her off with a dagger to the heart, and so she joined her mother and sisters in an honorable samurai death.

Unaware of his family's fate, Tanomo was captured in Hokkaido and then subsequently pardoned by the new government, which recognized his ability. Thereafter, Tanomo acted as Shinto priest and informal governmental adviser in various districts. In keeping with the spirit of the times, Tanomo decided that the superlative *oshiki-uchi* techniques which had served the Aizu warriors so well should be systematized and taught to the world at large.

When Tanomo realized that Sokaku was ill-suited to be a Shinto priest—the demon warrior was virtually illiterate, too intent on martial arts practice to waste time reading or writing—he began instructing his charge in *oshiki-uchi* techniques. Even then, Sokaku was Tanomo's second choice to be his successor.

Tanomo had initially imparted his teaching to his adopted—some say illegitimate—son Shiro (1872–1923). Shiro's talent later attracted the attention of Jigoro Kano, who immediately recruited the young martial artist for the newly established Kokodan Judo training hall. In 1887 an open match was held between representatives of the old and new styles of *jujutsu;* Shiro, utilizing techniques he had learned from Tanomo, defeated a huge opponent, carrying the day for Kano's group. Kano looked upon the able Shiro as his most promising disciple, and, as mentioned above, Tanomo also thought of the boy as his heir. Shiro had the makings of another Morihei, but in 1891, for reasons clear only to himself, Shiro abandoned the practice of both *oshiki-uchi* and *judo* and fled to distant Nagasaki to devote himself to journalism, politics, and Japanese archery. He resisted all attempts to have him resume the other two arts. Only when it was evident that Shiro was firm in his resolution did Tanomo finally settle on Sokaku as recipient of the *oshiki-uchi* techniques.

In the meantime, the peripatetic Sokaku was off again making the rounds to sharpen his fighting skills. Around 1877, he was reportedly in Kyushu, perhaps hoping to see action in the revolt led by Tanomo's relative Takamori Saigo. (Sokaku was still a child during the earlier Aizu revolt; if he had been a few years older, he would have been compelled to commit suicide with the famous Byakko-Tai, "Aizu's Boys' Army.") By the time he arrived, the rebellion had been quashed, so Sokaku created his own battles by storming local *dojo*s and earning spare change by taking on all comers at carnivals. After running out of opponents on Kyushu, Sokaku made his way to Okinawa, home of "empty-handed combat," thus adding karate to his list of mastered martial arts.

In short, Sokaku spent his youth as a "street fighter," engaging in hundreds of no-holds-barred fights to the finish. He killed a number of opponents and once waged a minor one-man war against a gang of construction workers. Sokaku got into an argument with the gang and drew his sword when they attacked him with axes, iron rods, and bricks. Sokaku slashed his way through the crowd, leaving many dead and wounded. He was arrested and charged with manslaughter but was later released when he was judged to have acted in self-defense. The authorities confiscated his sword, however, and warned him to avoid similar trouble in the future.

Sokaku's grim countenance was due to his lack of front teeth; he lost them during a demonstration against three men armed with spears. When Sokaku shattered one of the spears with his sword to impress the audience, the flying spear blade struck him in the mouth.

In 1880, Sokaku resumed his study with Tanomo at Nikko's Toshogu Shrine, where Tanomo had been appointed assistant priest. By 1888, the thirty-year-old Sokaku had begun to accept students of his own. In an attempt to lead a more normal life, Sokaku married and built a house; however, his wife died while giving birth to their second child and a fire destroyed his home shortly thereafter. Sokaku subsequently placed his children with relatives and once again assumed a wandering life.

It was not until 1899 that Tanomo taught Sokaku the last of the *oshiki-uchi* techniques, presenting him with this verse as a type of "certificate."

> *All people, know this!*
> *When you strike*
> *a flowing river*
> *no trace remains*
> *in the water.*

Between 1898 and 1915 when he met Morihei in Hokkaido, Sokaku traveled from place to place, mostly in northern Japan, making a living by conducting what we would call seminars and workshops. If Sokaku's records are to be believed, nearly all of the top martial artists of the era were, at one time or another, his students. In those days, "enrolling" in Sokaku's course meant losing a contest to him. Since so many of the defeated challengers were top instructors in their own right, it is an indication of Sokaku's great skill that he was able to beat his opponents regardless of what style they had trained in.

In 1904, Charles Perry, an American who taught English at Sendai Higher School, had a run-in with Sokaku on a train. Perry disliked the looks of a shabbily dressed Japanese passenger sharing his first-class car and asked the conductor to check the fellow's ticket. When Sokaku demanded to know why he alone was being asked to show his ticket, the conductor told him of the American gentleman's complaint. The enraged Sokaku jumped out of his seat and rushed over to Perry for an explanation. Perry leaped up, confident that his six-foot height would intimidate the diminutive Sokaku. Instead, Sokaku swiftly grabbed Perry's brandished fists, applied an excruciating pressure-point pin, and then threw Perry toward the back of the car. After recovering from the pain of the pin and the shock of being so easily handled by one half his size, Perry humbly apologized and asked to be taught the art. Through Perry, word of the efficacy of Sokaku's techniques reached the ears of President Theodore Roosevelt; Sokaku dispatched his disciple Shunso Harada, a police official from Sendai, to the United States, where he gave instruction to the American leader and other members of the government over a three-year period.

The following tale dates from the same period: in Fukushima Prefecture, a bandit was terrorizing the populace, but despite their best efforts, the police failed to apprehend him. One morning the outlaw was discovered dead in a field with his neck nearly wrenched off his shoulders. Everyone wondered who had dared to slay this vicious criminal. Officially, no one was named, but several policemen knew quite well

Daito Ryu Master Takeda Sokaku, even in his eighties as ferocious as ever.

that Sokaku, who was conducting a training session in the area at the time, deliberately walked alone along the darkest roads each night.

Around 1911, Sokaku was invited by the police bureau in Hokkaido to train its officers. In addition to legitimate settlers such as Morihei's group, the wide-open frontier of Hokkaido was a haven for brigands—pirates infested the coast and highwaymen roamed the interior. Gangs, prototypes of today's *yakuza,* ran smuggling, gambling, and slave labor operations. Police were largely powerless and outnumbered; several stations were in fact sacked by the gangs.

Much like a U.S. marshal called in to restore law and order to a wild cowtown, Sokaku, then in his fifties, made his way to the untamed wilderness. Gangsters, alerted to Sokaku's arrival, immediately put a tail on the tiny warrior. When they learned that he visited a public bath, unarmed, every morning, six hooligans were assigned to teach him a lesson. The snap of a wet towel can raise welts on bare flesh even in the hands of a schoolboy; when Sokaku projected his *ki* into the makeshift weapon, he knocked his attackers senseless or shattered their ribs. Terrified by Sokaku's unbelievable ability, a small army of two hundred gangsters surrounded Sokaku's hotel and prepared for a showdown. The defiant Sokaku vowed to strew the streets with dead bodies, and the town's citizens scrambled for cover. In the best tradition of a Hollywood western, a truce was arranged between the gang leader and Sokaku, and bloodshed was avoided.

When Sokaku returned to Hokkaido a few years later, inevitably he and Morihei crossed paths. Morihei had known of Sokaku's presence in Hokkaido for some time. Once, after thrashing a *sumo* wrestler in an impromptu contest, Morihei was asked if he was the "famous Sokaku Takeda." On a trip to Engaru, Morihei learned that Sokaku was conducting a session in a nearby inn and immediately rushed there to attend.

After witnessing an impressive demonstration and being deftly handled by the skinny Sokaku, Morihei applied for admission to the "Daito Ryu," as Sokaku styled his teaching, and was accepted. Morihei forgot about everything else, staying at the inn for a month, training day and night with Sokaku; following thirty days of practice, Morihei was presented with a first-level teaching license.

Morihei then returned to Shirataki—much to the relief of his family and friends; they had assumed that he had perished in a blizzard since they had not heard from him in a month. Then he built a *dojo* and house for Sokaku on his property, invited the master to teach there, and received private instruction each morning for two hours. Sokaku also taught a group lesson later in the day. Because Sokaku was a teacher of the old school, Morihei was obliged to wait on his master hand and foot, personally preparing Sokaku's meals, washing his clothes, endlessly massaging his shoulders and legs, and helping him bathe.

Following the great fire in Shirataki in 1917, Morihei had less time to train with

Sokaku, although he did continue to accompany him on occasional instruction tours to various parts of Hokkaido.

Morihei suddenly left Hokkaido for good at the end of 1919. The "official" reason for Morihei's flight from Shirataki is his father's critical illness back in Tanabe. This explanation has been questioned, however, and it seems certain that his father's sickness was a convenient excuse rather than the main cause of Morihei's departure.

First of all, prior to receiving news of his father's critical condition, Morihei had already sent his family (which now included two infant sons born in Hokkaido) back to Tanabe. Furthermore, he was obviously not content in Shirataki, unhesitatingly abandoning everything he owned there (the bulk of his property and possessions were turned over to Sokaku). Finally, he did not rush to his dying father's bedside but made a detour to visit the headquarters of the new Omoto-kyo religion. Even if his visit there was to pray for his father's recovery, it would have been more natural to return directly to Tanabe to assess the situation firsthand.

It is my view that Morihei was both spiritually restless, still searching for life's purpose, and disenchanted with Sokaku's teaching methods, anxious to experiment on his own, free of the ceaseless demands of that exacting and exasperating mentor.

Although Sokaku was undeniably an extraordinary martial artist, certainly one of the most talented *budoka* of all time, his character was not similarly advanced. Ill-tempered, vain, and arrogant, he was inordinately proud of the many men he had cut down (yet terrified of their departed spirits, which he said haunted him at night), and he constantly heaped scorn on other teachers and traditions. For example, he once referred to the dignified Jigoro Kano as a "fish peddler." When the violent Sokaku spied another human being, he saw an enemy; he carried an unsheathed dagger on his person whenever he stepped out, and his walking stick concealed a razor-sharp blade that he applied to any dog that dared bark at him. Even at home, he kept a pair of sharpened chopsticks at hand to repel any intruders. Insanely suspicious, Sokaku would not take any food or drink—even tea he prepared himself!—without having a disciple taste it first lest it be poisoned. It has also been rumored that the real reason that Morihei sent his family back to Tanabe is that Sokaku was making advances to Morihei's wife.

In any case, in 1919, the thirty-six-year-old Morihei found himself in Ayabe, a small town near Kyoto, where he had a fateful encounter with one of the most enigmatic figures of the twentieth century, Onisaburo Deguchi.

2

As THE OLD ORDER DISINTEGRATED in nineteenth-century Japan, there was a surge of hope that a new age would emerge from the chaos. Suddenly there were seers, prophets, and messiahs everywhere, each one proclaiming a way out of the fighting, disease, and hardship then engulfing their world.

Many of the founders of these new religious movements were women. Indeed, it was felt during this tumultuous period that it was pure-hearted women who were closest to the Divine—and not aristocratic ladies sheltered from the harsh realities of life but undereducated, desperately poor peasant women.

One of the most remarkable of these prophetesses was Nao Deguchi. Born in 1836 to an impoverished family during one of the worst famines in Japan's history, Nao miraculously escaped "thinning out"—the euphemism for infanticide, which was typically aimed at female babies. Tens of thousands of people starved to death in the Great Tempo Famine; for several years lush Japan had no spring—every blade of grass, every root and piece of grain, all the leaves and bark of trees, even old tatami mats were devoured by the famished hordes. Although Nao survived, throughout her life she was buffeted by an endless round of tragedies.

When she was ten years old, Nao's alcoholic father died and the young girl was sent out to work, slaving away as a maid, shop girl, and seamstress to help support her family. At seventeen, Nao was adopted into the Deguchi family by her aunt, a sullen lady who committed suicide two years later. Nao's first engagement was broken off and, at age twenty, another match was arranged with a man she did not love.

Since her new husband was a master carpenter, among the highest-paid craftsmen of the time, there was a glimmer of hope that Nao's fortune would improve. Sadly, her easygoing husband was addicted to saké and vaudeville; the combination of heavy drinking, late nights on the town, and injuries suffered on jobs took their toll, and eventually the man was an unemployed invalid. Instead of prospering, Nao's family fell deeper and deeper into debt, losing everything they owned.

Of the eleven children Nao bore between the ages of twenty and forty-seven, three died at birth, two went insane, one was killed in the Sino-Japanese War, one attempted suicide, and three ran away from home. After her husband's death when she was fifty-one years old, Nao was reduced to rag picking to eke out the meagerest of livings.

From her youth, Nao frequently heard "inner voices" and occasionally disappeared for days on end to fast and pray in the mountains. She was at this time under the influence of the Konko-kyo religion, a new sect founded by the peasant Bunjiro Kawate in 1859.

Kawate believed himself to be the incarnation of Tenchi-Kane-no-Kami (also known as Konjin); this previously obscure deity, once considered a wrathful *kami* of minor importance, was actually, Kawate claimed, the supreme god of love that would lead mankind into an era of peace and prosperity. The god's message, as interpreted by Kawate, was "Reform the world, heal the sick, and prepare for a new era."

In 1892 the fifty-seven-year-old Nao received a personal summons from that august deity himself. One night, Nao suddenly felt as if she were drifting among the clouds, her body as light and transparent as a feather; her wretched little room was filled with soft light and a lovely fragrance. "I am Konjin," she heard herself exclaim. At Konjin's direction, Nao neither ate nor slept for the next thirteen days as she continuously purified herself with cold-water ablutions to prepare herself for further instructions from the god.

Crying out the prophetic utterances of Konjin, Nao began attracting attention, some of it unwanted. After she had mumbled something about the world being purified by fire, the police suspected her of being the arsonist then terrorizing the district. She was taken into custody and released only when the real arsonist confessed. Following this incident, Konjin ordered the illiterate Nao to take dictation. Writing "automatically" in simple *kana* script, Nao eventually filled some 100,000 pages with notes called *Fudesaki* ("Writings") from Konjin.

News of Nao's clairvoyance and ability to heal illness got out, and a small group of followers gathered around her in Ayabe. Her initial group was under the umbrella of the Konko-kyo organization, but Nao was restless—Konjin had told her to expect a "messiah from the East."

In 1898 Nao was approached by a dapper young man named Kisaburo Ueda. Born near Kameoka in 1871, Ueda also came from a family that had fallen on hard times. Ueda's grandfather had gambled away most of the family's once-considerable holdings, and the household was desperately poor. Ueda was largely raised by his grandmother, an unusually well-educated woman for that period. She was a skilled poet and a keen student of the sacred science of *kotodama* (sound-spirit), having learned the subject from her father, the top expert of the day. (Later, Ueda claimed that he was actually the illegitimate son of an imperial prince.)

The boy's weak constitution and frequent illnesses delayed his entrance into school for three years, but his brilliance allowed him to catch up quickly and then to surpass all the others. Unfortunately, his classmates and even a teacher—who did not care to be corrected by one of his pupils—were jealous of Ueda's genius and cruelly teased and mistreated the young scholar. The tables were turned when Ueda was appointed assistant instructor at the tender age of twelve; however, the outspoken youth had difficulty getting along with his much older colleagues and subsequently resigned his position two years later.

Ueda returned home, working as a farmer, peddler, and day laborer to support himself. At night, he continued his study of literature and practiced calligraphy and painting. From the age of eighteen, Ueda began contributing verse and essays to literary journals. He was particularly good at *kyoka,* satirical "mad verse."

In his early twenties, Ueda studied veterinary and dairy science and then established a milk-products business. He expanded his liberal arts education by learning classical Japanese music and dance. Ueda was a community activist, not hesitant to oppose village elders if he felt there had been injustice. To some, Ueda was a champion of the poor and oppressed; to others he was a meddlesome troublemaker disturbing the status quo. Argumentative and a bit of a dandy, Ueda was a favorite target of the local toughs; he was attacked and brutally beaten more than once.

In 1897 Ueda lost his father and underwent a spiritual crisis. Depressed, harassed by bullies, involved with prostitutes, and drinking heavily, he ran from the village and sequestered himself in a cave on Mount Takakusa, determined to find the truth or perish in the attempt.

There, during a week-long fast, Ueda entered, he claimed, a divine trance and toured the cosmos; gods and buddhas taught the flighty young mystic all their secrets. Thus enlightened, Ueda descended the mountain ready to devote himself to the salvation of the world.

At first, Ueda did not get much of a response to his message. He was dismissed as just another demented prophet by the villagers, and even his own family was embarrassed by Ueda's rantings. His resolutely dissolute brother repeatedly smashed his altars and hurled stones at him when he tried to do purification rites in the river. The police got on him for "preaching without a license." Under pressure from the authorities, Ueda decided to establish his credentials.

Ueda initially studied with the noted spiritualist Otate Nagasawa, who was then a teacher on Mount Ontake, home of one of Japan's foremost mountain religions. Nagasawa was the main disciple of Shintoku Honda, the charismatic leader responsible for the revival of the ancient *chinkon-kishin* Shinto meditation technique.

Following several months of intense study with Nagasawa, Ueda was given permission to act as a *saniwa,* a kind of "psychic umpire" who decided cases of spirit possession. (Ueda was quite pleased to have been judged to now be an instrument of the great god Susano-o-no-mikoto, rather than the small-time *tengu* goblin that was instructing him previously.)

One day, while performing rites at a shrine, Ueda heard a voice telling him to go to the west because someone was awaiting his arrival there. Ueda immediately set out in that direction even though he had no idea whom he was supposed to meet. As he was sitting in a tea shop, the proprietress asked him his business.

"I'm a *saniwa*," Ueda announced.

"Oh, how fortunate!" the woman exclaimed. "My mother is a mouthpiece for the god Konjin, and she has told us that she is expecting a divine messenger from the east. We opened this tea shop to search for the messenger, hoping that he would stop here. By all means, you must be introduced to her."

It is impossible to imagine two people more unlike than Nao Deguchi and Kisaburo Ueda. Tiny old Nao was reserved, abstemious, and guileless; vibrant young Ueda was outgoing, full of gusto, and shrewd. Nao, a simple, frugal woman, shied away from the limelight; Ueda, a cosmopolitan scholar-artist-entrepreneur, craved it. Interestingly, in subsequent Omoto-kyo hagiography, Nao is described as "a man's spirit in a woman's body," while Ueda is thought of as "a woman's spirit in a man's body."

Despite the dramatic circumstances of their first encounter, it took both sides some time to conclude that the other party was the "real thing." After several months of wary negotiation, Nao and Ueda agreed to combine forces. Ueda moved to Ayabe, married Nao's sixteen-year-old daughter Sumi (born when her mother was forty-seven), and adopted the name Onisaburo (also read Wanisaburo) Deguchi.

Not long after his advent into the Deguchi family, Onisaburo attempted a takeover of the movement. He had big plans, but he ran into opposition from Nao's inner circle and then, from Nao herself, who complained bitterly about his bewildering innovations (including the "editing" of Nao's divinely inspired missives). In spite of a series of troubles—Nao's flight to a cave, Onisaburo's expulsion from the movement and assassination plots against him, lack of funds, and so on—Onisaburo's leadership prevailed. By 1913, Omoto-kyo emerged as an independent religious organization, and when Nao died in 1918, Onisaburo, the "Holy Guru," had total control of the movement.

Even though many of Onisaburo's theories and schemes were totally crackpot, he was clearly on a different plane than the other simple-minded religious cranks, deluded messiahs, and clever frauds that populated that era. In addition to possessing a brilliant mind, Onisaburo was an artist par excellence. His literary output is likely unequaled by anyone: he dictated over 600,000 poems and a number of books, including the incredible eighty-one volume *Reiki monogatari* ("*Tales of the Spiritual World*"). In this stupendous work—its outline alone runs to over 400 pages—Onisaburo roams the cosmos interpreting past, present, and future events in terms of *kotodama* theory as well as giving advice on more mundane matters, for example, the proper height of one's bed ("less than three feet high unless you are the emperor"), personal hygiene ("Men do not have an absolute right to enter a bath before women; it depends who is dirtier"), and marriage ("Couples should not be too much in love; otherwise they defer to each other, constantly avoiding the hard decisions necessary to maintain a household"). Onisaburo also tried his hand at playwriting, composing, movie directing, and sculpture, but he truly excelled at calligraphy, painting, and pottery. Regardless of what one thinks of his ideas, Onisaburo was undeniably one of East Asia's most gifted visual artists. His splendid free-flowing brushwork brought his characters and images to life, and his dramatic, brightly colored ceramics are rightly considered to rank with the "national treasures" of past masters.

Onisaburo was an effective spiritual teacher, soothing thousands with his *chinkon-kishin* meditation techniques. His prophecies were ambiguous enough to allow him to boast of a nearly perfect batting average, and he was, like many similar charismatic figures, good at curing psychosomatic illnesses. A master psychologist, Onisaburo was a skilled "mind-reader," sufficiently clairvoyant to disarm skeptics by, for example, telling them exactly how much money they had in their pockets. Unshakably optimistic, Onisaburo good-humoredly survived a series of setbacks that would have crushed the spirit of an ordinary mortal. He thought of himself as the modern version of the Shinto god Susano-o-no-mikoto, the mischievous deity forever in trouble because of his antics.

All of this, coupled with his majestic appearance—surrounded by a bevy of beautiful young women, clad in a resplendent kimono with a colorful shaman's hat over his piled-up mane of hair—made Onisaburo an indeed impressive, often irresistible leader. For the first time, a new religion began to attract intellectuals, aristocrats, government officials, and military men rather than merely disgruntled farmers and innocent country folk. Between 1919 and 1921, the "Golden Age of Omoto-kyo," membership reached several million, and millions more were directly influenced by Omoto-kyo publications, including a daily newspaper.

Even in remote Hokkaido, word of the exciting new religion headquartered in Ayabe reached Morihei's ears. When Morihei departed from Shirataki, he was not drawn to Tanabe but to Ayabe, where he came face to face with the Holy Guru himself.

As soon as Morihei stepped off the train at Ayabe station, he sensed something different—the entire area percolated with energy. The spectacle at the majestic Omoto-kyo headquarters took Morihei's breath away: scores of long-haired men and women, clad in bright kimonos and flowing skirts, bustling around huge halls and sacred ponds, resolved to "reform the world and create heaven on earth." Overwhelmed, Morihei found himself drawn toward the Dragon Pavilion. There he took a seat in a dimly lit

Flamboyant Onisaburo Deguchi, dressed in shaman's robes. Onisaburo had hundreds of magnificent outfits and once had himself photographed elaborately dressed up as, respectively, Miroku Buddha, the Shinto Deity Susano-o, and the seven folk gods of good fortune.

Ink painting of a pine tree by Onisaburo. "Art is the mother of religion" was a basic Omoto-kyo tenet, and Onisaburo was a highly skilled artist, excelling especially at brushwork and pottery. Venerable pines, symbols of everlasting life and eternal spring, were a favorite subject of Onisaburo's. Instead of using a regular seal, Onisaburo frequently stamped his pieces with his thumbprint near the top of the work, thereby "activating" it, a practice similar to the Tibetan custom of having a Grand Lama put his handprints on the back of a *thangka* to consecrate it.

corner and began softly reciting the Shingon chants and prayers he had years before committed to memory. Suddenly an apparition of his father appeared before him. Then another figure emerged from the darkness, saying, "What do you see?"

"My father," Morihei replied sadly. "He looks so old and wasted away."

"Your father is fine," Onisaburo gently said to Morihei. "Let him go."

Completely enthralled with the otherworldly air of Ayabe, Morihei lingered on for several more days, speaking to Onisaburo, learning about Omoto-kyo doctrine, and joining *chinkonkishin* meditation sessions.

When he finally returned to Tanabe, Morihei was shocked to find that his father had, as Onisaburo hinted, passed away peacefully. Morihei was informed of his father's last words to his temperamental yet beloved son: "Let nothing bind you—live the way you want."

For the next few months, Morihei behaved as if mad. He spoke to no one and passed each night alone in the mountains furiously swinging his sword. Then, to everyone's consternation, he unexpectedly announced his intention to move to Ayabe and join Omoto-kyo. His family and friends were aghast at the plan—Omoto-kyo had recently received a lot of bad press, and, as his wife complained, "Why leave this place when we have productive land and fine neighbors? Are the gods there that you say are calling you going to pay you a salary?"

Once Morihei's mind was made up, however, there was no turning back. In the spring of 1920, the thirty-seven-year-old Morihei, his wife and three children, and his mother made the move to Ayabe.

After settling in a small house near the main shrine (Morihei purchased, just before the move, a three-year supply of rice as a kind of insurance policy), Morihei assisted with the many farming and construction projects then in full swing as well as participating in the various prayer services, meditation sessions, special fasts, and purification ceremonies. He threw himself into the study of Omoto-kyo creeds and, after being taught by Onisaburo that art is the mother of religion, took up calligraphy and poetry composition.

Omoto-kyo regarded agriculture as the basis of the new world order and stressed natural farming methods and wholesome food. Animals were not kept at Ayabe, and since the use of human "night soil" was inappropriate for vegetables offered in the shrines, Omoto-kyo organic farmers developed a highly refined system of composting.

Throughout his life, Morihei was passionately fond of farming. With the abolition of feudalism, many former samurai rediscovered the affinity between *budo* and farming, two disciplines that promoted clean living and high thoughts. Morihei had extra-heavy tools forged for him and wielded his hoe with the same concentration and extension as his sword.

Morihei was in charge of composting and rose each day at 3:00 A.M. to collect waste material from a number of far-flung places. One day he cleared a field of kudzu and dragged an enormous clump of vines back along the road to Ayabe. On the way, a pedestrian accidentally got tangled in the vines, and Morihei, single-mindedly going full blast, covered another mile before finally hearing the poor fellow's cry for help.

Initially, Morihei practiced martial arts by himself in the evenings. After an Omoto-kyo fire brigade was organized, he directed the training drills, which included basic martial arts techniques. Onisaburo subsequently requested that Morihei teach *budo* to the other Omoto-kyo believers, partly to build character and partly to train a group of bodyguards. A building was remodeled to house the "Ueshiba Academy," Morihei's first *dojo*.

The present head of Omoto-kyo, Onisaburo's daughter Naohi, was one of Morihei's earliest students. "He made no allowances for women," she recalled, "and treated male and female the same during practice. It was hard on us girls, but we appreciated not being made to feel inferior because of our sex." While Morihei taught mostly practical self-defense to his trainees, he continued to research sword and spear movements on his own.

The opening of Morihei's first training hall was the only happy event of Morihei's first year in Ayabe. Within three weeks of each other, Morihei's two sons, aged three and one years old, died of illness (Morihei's sole surviving son, Kisshomaru, was born a year after his two brothers' deaths); and on February 11, 1921, Ayabe was hit by the First Omoto-kyo Incident.

For several years, the government had been monitoring Omoto-kyo activities with increasing suspicion. Overenthusiastic Omoto-kyo followers were spreading rumors that Nao had prophesied that there would be a war between Japan and the rest of the world no more than a few years in the future; that Japan, in its present state, would disappear and a new order emerge; and that the true emperor of Japan was not the sickly Taisho occupying the throne in Tokyo but the dynamic spiritual leader residing in Ayabe: Onisaburo was the one destined to establish a universal kingdom of peace and love.

Government spies and renegade Omoto-kyo members filed shocking reports: Nao's regal tomb was constructed in the manner reserved for emperors and empresses; Onisaburo's residence was modeled after that of the imperial palace; Omoto-kyo believers had stockpiled weapons, explosives, food and money on the Ayabe compound and were weaving an enormous "imperial flag" to rally behind when the revolution was launched; secret caves at the headquarters were filled with sex slaves and the dead bodies of those who dared cross Onisaburo and his minions.

Sufficiently alarmed, authorities ordered the police to raid Omoto-kyo headquarters. Onisaburo and several of his chief aides were arrested; when no weapons or bodies were discovered on the premises, the government was forced to limit its charges against Onisaburo to lese majesty and violation of the Newspaper Control Act. Onisaburo was imprisoned for several months and then released on bond; he was found guilty of lese majesty and given a five-year sentence, which he immediately appealed, remaining free on bond. However, upon his conviction, the government ordered the main Omoto-kyo buildings destroyed.

Unlike the more serious Second Omoto-kyo Incident ten years later, this first incident seems not to have greatly affected Morihei. As a brand-new member of Omoto-kyo, attracted to its spiritual message, Morihei was largely unaware of the political intrigue surrounding the controversial organization, and he had little to do with the promotional aspects of the movement. Despite the incident, Morihei remained an ardent believer in Omoto-kyo and a firm supporter of Onisaburo. In fact, following Onisaburo's release from prison, Morihei acted as Onisaburo's personal bodyguard and close confidant.

Onisaburo's conviction and the destruction of the Omoto-kyo buildings put a damper on things for the next two years. In that period Morihei devoted himself to farming, study, and martial arts training.

Early in the spring of 1922, Sokaku turned up at Ayabe with his wife and ten-year-old son (Sokaku had married a young girl in Hokkaido). Daito Ryu accounts state that

Morihei invited Sokaku to teach at the Omoto-kyo headquarters, but this is preposterous given the turmoil surrounding recent events there. Who would want such a difficult person around at a time like that? It appears that while in Hokkaido, Sokaku had heard rumors of an "Ueshiba Academy" in Ayabe and invited himself.

Even though Morihei was not charging for his lessons, Sokaku insisted that he organize special training sessions, to be led by Sokaku, for five yen a week. That was big money in those days, especially for a group of people deprived of much of their livelihood. As usual, Sokaku was terribly impressive despite his advanced age (mid-sixties), easily handling several previously "undefeated" swordsmen-members of Omoto-kyo. Onisaburo, on the other hand, took an immediate dislike to the cocky little brawler— "The man reeks of blood and violence"—and Sokaku refused to train with Morihei or teach him anything novel. In fact, Sokaku bitterly criticized Morihei for tampering with the Daito Ryu techniques.

Following a very tense six-month stay, Sokaku was finally persuaded to leave Ayabe when Morihei arranged for payment of an exorbitant "farewell gift." Since this money, the equivalent of nearly $10,000, was ostensibly presented to Sokaku's wife, it is not entered in the Daito Ryu official records. All that is found there is a note confirming Morihei's appointment as an Assistant Instructor and the receipt of a modest three-yen fee. (Sokaku's son has recently claimed that Morihei kept the money for himself and that Sokaku received nothing.)

Morihei would meet the exasperating Sokaku again, but it is clear that as early as 1922, Morihei was embarking on a separate course from that of the Daito Ryu teacher. Morihei was much more comfortable with Onisaburo.

Onisaburo was called many things during his eventful career, ranging from "Savior of the World" to "The Biggest Charlatan in History," but perhaps the title most apt was "The Ultimate Don Quixote." One of his favorite sayings was: "Form the sun, earth, and moon into a sweet cake, cover it with star dust, and swallow it whole!" Onisaburo was further convinced that he was an incarnation of Miroku, the Enlightened One scheduled to appear and usher in a golden age of peace and prosperity. It was this heartfelt belief that led Onisaburo to undertake "The Great Mongolian Adventure."

"Imperial Japan" was the theme of the times, and the goal of Japanese nationalists was the creation of a "Greater East Asian Co-prosperity Sphere." They particularly had their eyes on the vast, underpopulated, underdeveloped, but resource-rich plains of Manchuria and Mongolia. The nomads there were miserably poor, ignorant, and dominated by evil Buddhist lamas; Japan would magnanimously liberate the area from the Chinese, help Mongolian patriots form their own nation, and advise their brothers on the "proper" way to run the country.

To that end, countless secret societies and spy rings were operating in northern Asia. The largest and most notorious of these groups was the Black Dragon Society (or, more correctly, the Amur River Society), founded by the right-wing activist and martial artist Ryohei Ueda in 1901. Membership ranged from cabinet ministers and senior military officials to agent provocateurs, spies, and hired assassins.

In stark contrast to Europeans and Americans, who barely tolerated the disreputable business of spying and espionage as a necessary evil, the Japanese regarded intelligence gathering and counterespionage as highly patriotic acts to be proud of. The incredible dedication of the large number of high-ranking military officers, many of them from aristocratic families, who were willing to labor away for years posing as coolies, houseboys, cooks, and brothel keepers—or, in the case of female agents, as brothel inmates—simply to acquire scraps of information is beyond the comprehension of Westerners. Every Japanese in China was, in effect, a spy passing along whatever he or she had seen or heard. Organizations such as the Black Dragon Society even sponsored the religious pilgrimages of Buddhist monks, hoping to receive valuable firsthand intelligence regarding people and places normally off-limits to military personnel. (The renowned Ekai Kawaguchi, "the first Japanese in Tibet," was one such monk. Even though he was a serious Buddhist practitioner, his acute observations on the political situation in Tibet provided the Japanese secret police with much needed intelligence.)

Yutaro Yano, a retired naval commander and Omoto-kyo follower with links to the Black Dragon Society, invited Onisaburo to come to Mongolia, optimistic that the charismatic religious leader would win the people's confidence, thus paving the way for a smooth takeover by Japanese-supported Mongolian war lords.

For years, Onisaburo dreamed of becoming the spiritual and temporal leader of not just little Japan but the entire world. To facilitate communication between different branches of his future empire, Onisaburo enthusiastically promoted Esperanto and romanized Japanese as universal languages. Onisaburo made contacts with like-minded groups overseas that advocated the synthesis of world religions and the creation of an international government (Bahaism was one such group). When Yano's invitation arrived, Onisaburo—who was greatly influenced by the prediction of the Swedish mystic Emmanuel Swedenborg that a new Jerusalem was due to descend to earth in the East—believed that he was receiving a divine summons to spearhead the fashioning of a Heaven on Earth.

The ever-confident Onisaburo surreptitiously departed for the Chinese mainland in early February 1924. Accompanying him were a lawyer named Matsumura (a world government would need an attorney general right away to draw up a new legal code), a barber called Nada (the savior of mankind must be presentable at all times), Morihei (bodyguard extraordinaire and future commander of the spiritual army), and Yano. The group inconspicuously made their way through Korea, at that time under Japanese occupation, and then to Feng-tian. There they were met by their advance man Kitamura and several Black Dragon Society agents who would act as guide-interpreters.

The situation in that corner of Asia was chaotic: the young Chinese republic, only twelve years in existence, was engaged in a running battle with local war lords and bandit chiefs for control of the area; Japanese troops stationed nearby were eagerly awaiting a pretense that would allow them to invade Manchuria; and the Soviet Red Army was poised on the border of Outer Mongolia. The district was swarming with spies and espionage agents working on behalf of a score of domestic and foreign interests.

Yano was in cahoots with a Mongolian bandit chief called Lu. He urged Lu to form a coalition with Chang, the top warlord in the area, and to rebel against the Chinese central government, demanding the establishment of an independent Mongolian state. "We will help you secure material," Yano assured Lu, "and with the services of Onisaburo you will capture the people's hearts."

A meeting was arranged between Lu and Onisaburo; subsequently it was agreed, among other things, that the Omoto-kyo leader would head a kind of "Salvation Army" mission to Mongolia. Since Japanese Shinto was not a suitable religion in those circumstances, Onisaburo formulated, on the spot, Omoto Buddhism. He designated himself as the Maitreya Incarnation Dalai Lama (as opposed to the Avalokiteshvara Incarnation Dalai Lama in Tibet); Matsumura, the second in command, was nominated as the Panchen Lama. All members took regal Chinese monikers as well. Morihei's was Wang Shou-kao, King of Protectors.

Superstitious, naive, and stubborn, Lu was a very poor choice as a collaborator in such a grand scheme. He was totally dazzled by Onisaburo—the physiognomists and soothsayers he had secretly retained to evaluate the Omoto-kyo Patriarch reported that not only did the Japanese lama possess the thirty-three marks of a living buddha, but he had a star-shaped birthmark on his back and the stigmata to boot! Thus Lu was absolutely certain that this messiah would lead them all to the promised land. Furthermore, he could not discern that Chang was merely pretending to support his cause; Lu would dig his own grave, Chang correctly calculated, and Chang would be free of a pesky rival.

The ill-fated party started out for Mongolia at the beginning of March. They received the honor of being loaned two of the very few automobiles in the entire province. Unfortunately, paved roads were not part of the bargain, and the group would have made faster progress on foot over the endless procession of rocky roads, muddy fields, and icy rivers that awaited them. After experiencing innumerable breakdowns, dreadful weather, and continual harassment by local authorities, police, and army patrols, the party arrived at the border town of Taonan. Following a brief rest and consultation with the Japanese agents operating there, they proceeded toward the Mongolian holy city of Ulanhot.

As an ancient center of Tantric Buddhism, Ulanhot was the perfect place for Onisaburo's flamboyant style of religion. He made his entrance on a snow-white horse, and lay folk and lamas alike were captivated by his lordly presence and grand manner of conducting prayer services and meditation ritual. In addition to his skill as a psychologist and mind-reader, Onisaburo's knowledge of medicine—he had once studied veterinary science—put him in good stead healing the painful but essentially minor illnesses that plagued the populace and their livestock.

A rumor, no doubt encouraged by Onisaburo, circulated that the lama was in fact a Mongolian, not a Japanese. Soon after his birth, Onisaburo's Mongolian father died and his mother married a Japanese, who subsequently took his family to that country; Onisaburo had now returned to his homeland, as a second Genghis Khan, to guide his fellow Mongols to independence.

On his part, Onisaburo was enthralled with the unlimited vistas of the Mongolian landscape. When he visited the Great Kingan Range he was moved to compose this verse:

> *Heaven? Earth?*
> *Or the vast sea?*
> *I cannot tell—*
> *pure moonbeams over*
> *the vast plains of Mongolia.*

Morihei, too, became an instant lama, giving lavish performances of *chinkon-kishin* techniques and applying the laying on of hands to cure illness. When he demonstrated his prowess as the King of Protectors by causing powerfully built Mongol warriors to collapse by merely touching them—the ignorant fighters were unaware that he attacked their vital pressure points—word spread that Morihei was a frightful sorcerer. Morihei gave formal instruction to selected military men and also learned a great deal about continental fighting arts in the process.

Even though Onisaburo and Morihei were received enthusiastically by the general public, skeptical war lords wanted more proof of the Grand Lama's divinity before committing themselves unreservedly to Lu's cause.

"How about conjuring up a rainstorm?" Lu said to Onisaburo. "That shouldn't be too difficult for a living buddha."

Onisaburo was reluctant, but Matsumura volunteered to act as his proxy. The two secluded themselves for a week to prepare for the important event. On the scheduled day, the two were taken to a parade ground where a large crowd had gathered to see if the two lamas had what it takes. As an added challenge there was not a single cloud in the deep-blue Mongolian sky. Inexplicably, Matsumura managed to pray up a storm—clouds rose out of nowhere, thunder roared, and the rain came pouring down. When the photographer sighed, "Well, I guess that ruins today's commemorative picture," Onisaburo leaped up, went out into the middle of the field, raised his arms to heaven, and let loose with a tremendous shout. The wind died down, the sky cleared, the sun returned, and the photograph was taken.

However impressive, even this performance did not stem the tide beating against Lu and his forces. The arms promised by Yano failed to materialize, and Chang denounced Lu's plot to the government. As the Chinese army began pressing in on the rebel, Lu decided to set up a different base in the southern town of Baian Dalai. Onisaburo, alerted by his "divine messenger service," warned Lu of the danger awaiting the war lord there. "If we are attacked," Lu countered, "Your Holiness can call down a flood and drown our enemies."

Faced with no alternative, the Japanese group reluctantly accompanied Lu to Baian Dalai. Ambushed several times, the party miraculously survived, finally arriving at the gates of Baian Dalai. Much to their chagrin, they were arrested and bound, and had their valuables confiscated (including Onisaburo's platinum watch, his priceless Japanese sword, and a small fortune in gold) by the authorities there. A few hours later they were unexpectedly released and taken to spend the night at the town's best inn.

Lu and his lieutenants were there too; the entire group was wined and dined, and women were brought in for the soldiers. A special bath was prepared, and everyone was treated to a shave and haircut. Despite the lavish treatment, Onisaburo and Lu were grim—they knew that it was an old Chinese custom to fete condemned prisoners the night before their execution.

Early in the morning, Lu and his men, 130 in all, were roused one by one and shot. Perhaps alerted to Morihei's reputation as a superlative bodyguard, a large contingent of soldiers, their weapons drawn, burst into the rooms housing the Japanese. The men were cast into leg and arm irons and paraded to the execution grounds.

Onisaburo and his companions were calm, almost jovial, considering their dire straits. "After we are killed, be sure to keep your souls close to mine so I can direct you to paradise," Onisaburo counseled Morihei and the rest of the members. Since the other men were not much good at poetry, Onisaburo composed "farewell verses" for all of them. Perhaps the most stirring was this one:

> *Even though our bodies*
> *will wither away here*
> *on the plains of Mongolia,*
> *our deeds as Japanese patriots*
> *will never fade.*

At this dramatic juncture, according to Omoto-kyo versions, a messenger arrived with word of a last-minute reprieve. Actually, it is almost certain that the Chinese had no intention of carrying out their threat of execution. The long delay between the killings of Lu's men and the execution of the Japanese party was ascribed implausibly to "faulty weapons." Surely, the Chinese army could have found at least one weapon in working order in their arsenal if they truly wanted to dispose of Onisaburo's group. At the time, the risk of Japanese intervention was too great, and the Chinese would not want to provoke an incident by executing Japanese nationals, even spies. In fact, as noted above, unlike Western powers, which rarely admitted publicly to fielding agents, the Japanese were quick to defend their "heroes" by whatever means necessary. The Chinese were apparently bluffing and released their prisoners into the custody of the local Japanese consul a few days after their capture.

Under Japanese military escort, Onisaburo and Morihei returned to Japan at the end of July. Onisaburo's bond was revoked, and he was imprisoned again, only to be released by November. (Remarkably, Onisaburo was permitted to visit China the following year to attend an international religious conference in Peking. To be sure, Onisaburo

Onisaburo and his group in leg irons following their capture by the Chinese army during the Great Mongolian Adventure. This was apparently a "memorial" photograph taken just before their release in custody of the Japanese consul. Matsumura is on the left, then Onisaburo, forty-one-year-old Morihei, a fellow named Ogiwara, and then two *agents provocateurs*, Inoue and Sakamoto. Kenkichi Inoue was in the employ of the Japanese Secret Service and likely a Black Dragon Society member as well. He engaged in espionage in Siberia before joining up with Onisaburo in Manchuria and later moved his base of operations to Peking, where he worked for, and spied on, the Ko-manji-kyo, a syncretic religion with close ties to Omoto-kyo. Morihei, fortunately, went on to better things after his escape.

had many enemies, but he also must have had many powerful supporters in high places to have been permitted so much freedom.) Onisaburo was typically unfazed by the debacle—"The timing must not have been right," he exclaimed—but Morihei was more than a little bitter about the manner in which the Omoto-kyo leader was "used" by political factions to advance their own interests.

Not surprisingly, Morihei was radically altered by his many face-to-face encounters with death during the Great Mongolian Adventure. He was particularly affected by this incident: "As we neared Baian Dalai we were trapped in a valley and showered with bullets. Miraculously, I could sense the direction of the projectiles—beams of light indicated their paths of flight—and I was able to dodge the bullets. The ability to sense an attack is what the ancient masters of the martial arts meant by 'anticipation.' If one's mind is steady and pure, one can immediately perceive aggression and counter it—that, I realized, is the essence of *aiki*."

Although Morihei's profound experiences in Mongolia made him a more considerate, less gruff person in social situations, he intensified his training in the martial arts, arming his disciples with live blades and instructing them to attack full force. Morihei also secluded himself deep in the mountains of his native Kumano to engage in the secret practices of Kuki Shinto. This ancient form of ascetic training includes long prayer fasts, purification in the sacred Nachi waterfalls, and "interiorization" of martial arts techniques.

Back again at Ayabe, strange things began to stir. Every evening Morihei's wife would hear an eerie *saaaaa* sound drifting down from the mountains where her husband was training. (There, Omoto-kyo believers were convinced, Morihei was being taught swordsmanship by a ferocious *tengu* gremlin.) In the morning, the high grass near Morihei's house was parted and bent as if some huge beast had passed through. During the day, the household altar would rattle and roll, emitting high-pitched noises.

In the spring of 1925, forty-two-year-old Morihei was transformed by a divine vision. Morihei gave different accounts of the event over the years, and, in his old age, seems to have gradually fused several separate incidents together to form this final version:

One day a naval officer visiting Ayabe decided to challenge Morihei to a *kendo* match. Morihei consented but remained unarmed. The officer, a high-ranking swordsman, was naturally offended at this affront to his ability and lashed out at Morihei furiously. Morihei easily escaped the officer's repeated blows and thrusts. When the exhausted officer finally conceded defeat, he asked Morihei his secret.

"Just prior to your attacks, a beam of light flashed before my eyes, revealing the intended direction."

Following the contest, Morihei went out to his garden to draw water from the well to wash the sweat from his face and hands. Suddenly Morihei started to tremble and then felt immobilized. The ground beneath his feet began to shake, and he was bathed with rays of pure light streaming down from heaven. A golden mist engulfed his body, causing his petty conceit to vanish, and he himself assumed the form of a Golden Being. Morihei perceived the inner workings of the cosmos and further perceived that "I am the Universe!" The barrier between the material, hidden, and divine worlds crumbled; simultaneously Morihei verified that the heart of *budo* was not contention but rather love, a love that fosters and protects all things.

This overwhelming experience was of course related to Morihei's Omoto-kyo beliefs; "unification with the Divine" was a central tenet of the faith, and Morihei was expressing his tremendous transformation in the only language he knew. Regardless of whether we take Morihei's statement at face value or explain his enlightenment more "rationally" as the result of supreme effort, superhuman strength, and natural ability, Morihei was undoubtedly a changed man thereafter. His sixth sense of anticipation was completely developed, and he was now invincible as a martial artist.

3

FOLLOWING MORIHEI'S ENLIGHTENMENT EXPERIENCE, Omoto-kyo psychics swore that they saw rays emanating from his body; he was also capable of leaping incredible distances, up and over an attacker, and displacing enormously heavy boulders. Morihei could even dodge bullets fired at point-blank range. Once a group of Omoto-kyo-affiliated military officers formed a firing squad at Morihei's direction and aimed their pistols squarely at his heart. The instant that they pulled the triggers, Morihei gave out a tremendous shout and knocked them all flat on their backs.

Such amazing strength as Morihei now possessed began to attract attention outside of Omoto-kyo circles.

In addition to the military people who came to study at Ayabe with Morihei, a number of college athletes came up from Tokyo to challenge "Japan's Number One Martial Artist." When rugged Shutaro Nishimura, a member of Waseda University's famed *judo* club, heard Onisaburo describe Morihei as the greatest martial artist alive, he immediately requested an introduction. Upon meeting Morihei for the first time, Nishimura thought to himself, "Is this some kind of joke? How can this middle-aged country bumpkin be the strongest man in Japan?" As soon as the confident Nishimura moved toward Morihei, he suddenly, much to his surprise, found himself on his rear end. Morihei folded a piece of paper and waved it in front of Nishimura's startled face. "Grab it if you can!" Morihei challenged.

No matter how quickly Nishimura moved, he could not catch the piece of paper; on the contrary, he was continually spun to the ground. A final all-out attack also failed—Nishimura looked up from the mat at a smiling Morihei and wondered, "Can there really be a martial art in which one downs his attacker with a laugh?"

Nishimura introduced many of his fellow *judoka* to Morihei, including Kenji Tomiki, who was to become one of Japan's top martial artists. Tomiki once remarked, "I faced virtually every outstanding *judo* and *jujutsu* man in my career, but not one of them could hold a candle to Morihei. He was far and above the best, likely the most gifted master of all time." The ease with which Morihei's women students handled mashers and drunks helped spread the word among female practitioners.

In the fall of 1925, the distinguished admiral Isamu Takeshita arranged for Morihei to give a special demonstration in Tokyo before a select group of influential people. Morihei performed mostly spear techniques, and when asked what school he was affiliated with, he replied that his style was "natural form, independently developed."

One of the spectators stated, "In the old days, it is said that Genba Tawarabashi could lift and toss twenty sacks of rice with his spear in rapid succession. Can you do likewise?"

"Let's see," replied Morihei.

Twenty 125-pound sacks were carried into the garden (the demonstration was being held at a huge private mansion). The sacks were divided up into two piles facing east and west. Morihei alternately speared the top of the sacks in each pile, lifted them up, and then tossed them, without spilling a single grain, into two neat piles facing north and south.

After this impressive performance, Count Yamamoto, a former prime minister, requested that Morihei conduct a twenty-one-day training session at Aoyama Palace for members of the imperial family and their bodyguards. The training session proceeded smoothly the first week, but then several government officials, concerned that Morihei was an Omoto-kyo "secret agent," protested. Although Yamamoto and other senior statesmen vouched for Morihei, he himself was so peeved by the accusation that he canceled the remaining lessons and announced in an indignant huff, "I'm returning to Ayabe to resume farming."

Morihei went back to Ayabe, and in the spring of 1926, Admiral Takeshita again persuaded him to come to Tokyo, assuring him that there would be no further "misunderstandings." Morihei, not fully convinced, reluctantly agreed. After his arrival in the capital, he stayed briefly at the home of a business tycoon in the Yotsuya section of Tokyo and then at a small *dojo* on the property of another magnate in Shinagawa.

Morihei, however, was not well. One day he collapsed after training and appeared to be near death. While unconscious, Morihei experienced another vision, this time of a lovely rainbow-clad maiden riding on a heavenly tortoise; he interpreted this as an omen of divine favor.

His doctors thought otherwise and pronounced his condition terminal. Even though Morihei did not have stomach cancer as feared, bleeding ulcers and extreme exhaustion made his health precarious. Onisaburo met with Morihei in Tokyo and, alarmed at his trusted disciple's ghastly complexion, solicitously ordered him back to Ayabe to recuperate. Immediately after speaking to Onisaburo—who was under constant police surveillance—Morihei was accosted by two plainclothesmen and taken to police headquarters.

"One of your disciples is a dangerous right-wing radical," Morihei was told. "What do you know about him?" the police demanded.

"Nothing," Morihei responded honestly. "I've broken no laws. Why are you treating me like this?" Morihei was released but, physically ill and sick of such rude treatment, returned to his family in Ayabe.

Six months later, Takeshita and Morihei's other supporters were at Ayabe again, pleading with Morihei to settle permanently in Tokyo. Onisaburo gave Morihei his blessing—"*Budo* will be your *yusai,* a practice to manifest the divine"—and Morihei, determined the make the move final, took his wife and children with him this third trip.

A nice house was secured for them in the Shiba Shirogane section of Tokyo, but unfortunately Morihei lost his wallet somewhere between Ayabe and Tokyo, and the family arrived penniless. Morihei, too proud to tell anyone about the predicament, said nothing. Luckily, an observant acquaintance noticed the shortfall and learned the reason for the lack of cash. Adequate provisions were immediately provided.

A temporary *dojo* was constructed in a remodeled billiard room in the mansion of Duke Shimazu. Within a year, the family was obliged to move to larger quarters in Shiba Mita and then again to a bigger place in Shiba Kuruma, next to the famous Sangakuji, burial site of the "Forty-seven Ronin." When it became clear that makeshift *dojo*s could no longer handle the crush of trainees—people had to line up and wait for a turn on the mat—some of Morihei's wealthy supporters drew up plans for the construction of a large training hall. Land was acquired in the Wakamatsu district and a building fund was established.

While the *dojo* was being built, Morihei and his family leased a house in Mejiro. There he had two memorable encounters.

The first was with General Miura, a hero of the Russo-Japanese War. Miura was famed for cutting down over fifty Russian soldiers with his officer's sword despite having been pierced completely through the chest by a Russian bayonet. Miura had also been a student of Sokaku's and was interested in discovering whether Morihei was authentic.

After an exchange of pleasantries, Miura asked for a demonstration. Absolutely fearless and secretly harboring a desire to humiliate the upstart Morihei, the general attacked with all his might. In spite of his steely determination and martial prowess, Miura—like all challengers—was totally dominated by Morihei. Miura apologized for his rash behavior and begged to be admitted as a student: "Your techniques are a world apart from those of the Daito Ryu. It is true *budo.* Please enroll me as your disciple."

Even though Morihei could handle Miura with no difficulty, the general still wondered how well Morihei would fare against a no-holds-barred multiple attack. Miura eventually arranged for a demonstration by Morihei to be given at the Toyama Military Academy. After the demonstration, Miura informed Morihei that the cadets wanted a full display of his power.

"Is that so?" said Morihei as he scooped up the nearest cadet in one hand and lifted him high in the air. Morihei then placed his hand on Miura's shoulder and shouted to the cadets to straddle his outstretched arm. Eight piled on until there was room for no more.

Urged on by Miura, the cocky cadets challenged Morihei with wooden bayonets. They counseled him to wear protective armor, but Morihei refused: "It won't be necessary. Are you going to attack one at time?"

"Of course!"

"That is too easy. In my *budo,* we expect attackers from all directions. Come at me together!"

Hesitant as they were at first, only one cadet stepped forward. After he went flying, the cadets lost all reserve and rushed in, only to find themselves upended in a flash.

Jigoro Kano, the founder of Kokodan Judo, paid a visit to the Mejiro *dojo* in October 1930. Kano, a cosmopolitan, English-speaking intellectual, was in most respects the diametrical opposite of the old-fashioned mystic Morihei, but he too was dazzled by Morihei's techniques. "This is the ideal *budo*—true *judo,*" Kano exclaimed after witnessing Morihei's performance. Kano humbly asked Morihei to accept two of his senior students as trainees; Morihei agreed and Kano had them report to him regularly the results of their study with the master. There is another story that Kano and Morihei met again and after Morihei toyed with four or five of Kano's best students he asked the Judo Patriarch rather sharply, "Just what kind of *budo* are you teaching at the Kobukan?"

Somewhat sheepishly, Kano replied, "Our system is more a form of physical education than pure *budo.*"

Interestingly, although they were reportedly on good terms in later years, Morihei at that time refused to show anything to Kyuzo Mifune, Kano's chief instructor, lest he "steal" the techniques. Men who have trained with both teachers note that their movements were quite similar, so evidently Morihei had reason for concern.

The opening ceremony for the new *dojo* was held in April of 1931. It was crowned the Kobukan, Imperial Martial Valor Hall. *Imperial* refers to the "Imperial Way," promoted by, among others, Omoto-kyo; the Divine Land of Japan, it was thought, would lead the world from the darkness of chaos to the light of salvation.

The following summer the Society for the Promotion of Japanese Martial Arts (Dai Nihon Budo Senyo Kai) was established under the auspices of the Omoto-kyo organization, with Morihei acting as chief instructor. The main *dojo* of this society was located in Takeda, a mountain village in Hyogo Prefecture. An abandoned saké brewery was turned into a boot camp to train the rapidly expanding Omoto-kyo People's Militia. Morihei instructed there during the summers.

Morihei recruited members for the Budo Senyo Kai at Omoto-kyo gatherings by proclaiming, "You young fellows these days have no starch. If any of you think you can

Morihei, around age fifty, at his physical peak. In the prewar period, the hard-edged martial aspect of his character was dominant, as seen here—severe, solid, and intent. Morihei's sharp, penetrating gaze serves notice that he is ready for anyone foolish enough to attack.

take me on, come up here." Invariably, four or five youngsters would leap to the challenge and join the organization after being thrown across the room by Morihei.

The training at remote Takeda was particularly severe, each day full of roughhouse martial arts practice and heavy farmwork. It was an all-or-nothing, do-or-die atmosphere at Takeda, and soon there was a breach between the fervent Omoto-kyo believers preparing for a holy war and the non-Omoto-kyo instructors who did not share the faith. Morihei was more or less able to defuse the explosive situation, but things thereafter remained tense.

In addition to teaching at the Kobukan, Takeda, and various branch *dojo*s, Morihei instructed at the Toyama Academy, the Naval Academy, the Military Staff College, and the Military Police Academy.

Finally settled in Tokyo, Morihei became the center of a whirl of activity. Trainees clamored to be accepted as students, and Morihei was highly selective, requiring a proper introduction, two responsible sponsors, and, most important, a personal interview. If Morihei did not like what he saw, the candidate was immediately rejected without explanation. If, on the other hand, Morihei perceived that the petitioner was sincere, he accepted him or her unconditionally. There was no set system of fees, but every live-in disciple offered some type of payment, whether in the form of cash, food, supplies, or work. Practice sessions ran from six to seven and nine to ten in the morning, plus two to four in the afternoon and seven to eight in the evening.

The live-in disciples slept in the *dojo,* took care of the cleaning and other chores, and served as Morihei's attendants. Live-in disciples had to be literally on guard at all times. If Morihei caught them out of position—for example, talking on the telephone too intently, or entering a room or turning a corner without the proper caution—they received a sharp reprimand.

Although the following incident occurred after the war, it illustrates Morihei's dictum that training is a twenty-four-hour affair. The chief instructor of the Headquarters Dojo returned from an overseas tour with a flashy leather jacket, at the time a valuable object unattainable in Japan. It was stolen from the locker room, and the irate instructor summoned all the live-in trainees to denounce them for their unpardonable inattentiveness. Morihei strolled in and wanted to know the reason for the commotion. When he was told what happened, Morihei said, "Stolen, was it?," and walked silently around the group of seated disciples. Suddenly Morihei barked at the chief instructor, "It is *you* that is at fault." So saying, Morihei turned his back and left the hall, leaving everyone behind to ponder the meaning of his words. Later, one of the disciples, still puzzled by Morihei's remark, asked the master to explain.

"Don't you see? A martial artist should never be a show-off or attached to material possessions. That kind of attitude creates 'openings' both in oneself and in others. The chief instructor let his possessiveness get the better of him, and look what resulted."

Morihei with his wife, Hatsu, his sole surviving son, Kisshomaru, and one of his nieces, standing before his home in Tokyo sometime in the late 1930s.

Since Morihei was continually experimenting with new forms and developing novel techniques, there was no systematic, step-by-step instruction. The trainees worked on whatever Morihei happened to be researching at the moment. One disciple recalls that Morihei dreamed up new techniques in his sleep because he would sometimes rouse them at two o'clock in the morning to try out his latest innovations!

Morihei was also engaged in the study of sword techniques during this period at the Kobukan, going so far as to set up a separate *kendo* division. Morihei's adopted son (and son-in-law), Kiyoshi Nakakura, number-one disciple of the famous *kendo* master Hakudo Nakayama, led the *kendo* training. (Nakakura's lack of enthusiasm for his father-in-law's Omoto-kyo beliefs coupled with unresolved marital problems caused him to leave the Ueshiba family within a few years of his adoption.)

Early trainees at the Kobukan included Yoichiro Inoue, a relative raised by the Ueshiba family, who was physically a carbon copy of Morihei. Although Inoue likely knows more about the early career and techniques of Morihei than any other individual, this hard-drinking, uncommunicative man keeps to himself, heading a small martial art school called Shinei Taido. A similar figure was the herculean Tsutomu Yukawa, next to Morihei the strongest man at the Kobukan. Yukawa could bend nails with his bare hands and hoist a thick beam with two men standing on it. Unfortunately, Yukawa, a wild drinker, was bayoneted to death in a barroom brawl in Osaka during the war. Kenji Tomiki and Minoru Mochizuki were infatuated with Morihei's techniques but never abandoned their allegiance to Jigoro Kano. Both men (Tomiki died in the early 1980s) founded independent systems, combining elements of Judo, Aikido, and, in the case of Mochizuki, *karate* and *kendo*. Hajime Iwata and Rinjiro Shirata were two *judoka* who wholeheartedly embraced Aiki-budo. Iwata is still active today in the Osaka area; the highly respected Shirata, the "Marvel of the Kobukan," is perhaps the only instructor who has successfully integrated both the prewar and postwar styles of Aikido.

Special mention must be made of Takako Kunigoshi. This lively young woman trained on the same basis as the men, asking for and giving no quarter. She was frequently called on by Morihei to serve as his bag-carrier and partner for demonstrations and to illustrate the effectiveness of Kobukan techniques against male challengers. A high school principal who was so impressed by her graceful demeanor and striking composure as she swept the grounds of a shrine asked her, "Where did you learn to move like that?" When she informed him, "At the Kobukan," he immediately decided to have his best *judo* competitor, a young man named Gozo Shioda, sent there. Shioda went on to become one of Morihei's chief disciples, establishing his own independent Yoshinkan of hard-hitting, old-style Aikido.

Morihei's fame was such in the capital that he was summoned to give a command performance before Emperor Hirohito. Morihei at first declined, citing the following reason: "I cannot display false techniques in front of His Majesty. In actual combat, my opponents would never be able to spring up and attack me again—they would be killed in one fell swoop." Morihei's sentiments were relayed to the emperor, who subsequently replied that while he understood Morihei's position, he still would appreciate being shown Morihei's art demonstrated in the usual fashion.

The week before the scheduled demonstration Morihei was stricken with a severe gastrointestinal ailment; he vomited continuously and was extremely dehydrated by the day of the demonstration. Despite his grave condition, Morihei refused to cancel the appearance. As they carried him to the hall and helped him into his training outfit, the two disciples accompanying Morihei, Yukawa and Shioda, looked at the deadly-pale, emaciated face of their teacher and wondered, "How can he possibly give a demonstration in this state? He will never survive."

However, as soon as Morihei entered the presence of the emperor, he suddenly straightened up and strode briskly toward the center of the hall. Yukawa, afraid that his teacher was only functioning at one-tenth his normal strength, held back when he initiated his attack. With his guard down, Yukawa fractured his arm when Morihei threw him with the customary force. Shioda therefore had to take all the breakfalls for the entire forty-minute demonstration. Once out of the hall, all three collapsed and spent the rest of the week recovering in bed.

Before relating the birth of Aikido, I would like to summarize Morihei's relationships to the two major influences in his life: Sokaku Takeda and Onisaburo Deguchi.

As indicated earlier, the relationship between Sokaku and Morihei was strained almost from the start. Sokaku's son Tokimune, who currently heads the Daito Ryu, has written of his father's tender affection toward Morihei, but the truth of the matter is that Sokaku was terribly jealous of Morihei; he raided Morihei's *dojo*s for students—"Train with *me,* the real Daito Ryu master"—and, in effect, extorted money from his best pupil. Sokaku invited himself to the Kobukan not long after it was opened to present Morihei with a certificate he did not need or want. The charge listed for the license in the official records is modest, but Morihei was obliged to cover all of Sokaku's expenses as well as offer a substantial "thank-you" gift of money. Morihei often complained that he had, in effect, paid hundreds of dollars for each of the techniques that he had learned from Sokaku.

While Morihei's behavior toward his former teacher was impeccable, the people at Omoto-kyo and later at the Kobukan were keenly aware of Morihei's consternation at Sokaku's unwanted visits. Almost without exception (a notable one is Takuma Hisa, who bolted from Morihei's group to study with Sokaku), the irascible little tyrant made a highly unfavorable impression on all of Morihei's friends and disciples. Morihei had long before surpassed Sokaku as a martial artist, as one of the early disciples related: "Sokaku never attempted to instruct at the Kobukan but one evening demonstrated the 'correct' method of applying an arm pin to several of us live-in disciples. I pretended that the pin was effective, but it was not painful in the least and I could have easily resisted or countered it—something that never occurred with Ueshiba Sensei."

Initially, Morihei—essentially a self-taught master—used his Daito Ryu licenses to give himself a measure of legitimacy in document-obsessed Japan. After Sokaku's last visit to the Kobukan, Morihei removed his Daito Ryu licenses from the training hall and had nothing more to do with the old-time warrior. (Sokaku continued his itinerant life, passing away in 1943 at age eighty-three.)

Morihei's relationship with Onisaburo was much richer and far more positive. He was devoted to the Great Guru, and after sharing so many adventures together, these two eccentric, extraordinarily gifted men had a deep appreciation for each other's abilities. Morihei and Onisaburo were on the same spiritual wavelength; as it will be shown in Part Three, the philosophy of Aikido is firmly rooted in the teachings of Omoto-kyo—indeed, the two systems are largely interchangeable. Morihei remained a true believer in Omoto-kyo teachings throughout his life and maintained that it was Onisaburo who showed him the light.

Despite their natural affinity, both men felt compelled to eventually steer separate courses. After Morihei left Ayabe permanently in 1929—with the blessings and encouragement of Onisaburo—he broadened his contacts and dedicated himself to formulating his own unique "Way," independent of both the Daito Ryu and Omoto-kyo frameworks.

The loosening of ties to Omoto-kyo was fortuitous. The government would have probably indulged Onisaburo's fantasies if he had limited his shenanigans to Ayabe. However, Omoto-kyo's formation of quasi-military associations, its stockpiling of arms, and its links to ultra-right-wing groups, coupled with Onisaburo's public appearances in full imperial regalia, prompted the alarmed authorities to take action.

On the morning of December 8, 1935, five hundred heavily armed police officers stormed the main Omoto-kyo centers and arrested Onisaburo and his chief aides on charges of lese majesty and fomenting armed rebellion. Morihei, too, was a prime target of the crackdown.

As mentioned earlier, Morihei, as a prominent Omoto-kyo member, was under surveillance, and government agents once attempted to place a "mole" in the Kobukan. A man, purportedly with an introduction from Jigoro Kano, asked permission to become a live-in disciple. Morihei, who saw through the imposter, replied, "Only if you can defeat my newest trainee."

Morihei went out to talk with the novice who was sweeping the garden. He explained the situation and then taught the beginner a special technique.

"Use this technique," Morihei advised, "but if you do not execute it at the risk of your life, it will be ineffective."

The novice applied the technique as if there were no tomorrow and downed his opponent. As the humiliated challenger was about to depart, Morihei nonchalantly asked, "Who instructed you to spy on me?"

Following the establishment of the Budo Senyo Kai, Morihei came under even more scrutiny and a warrant was issued for his arrest by the Kyoto Police Headquarters on December 8.

Morihei, almost certainly alerted to the impending raid by his associates in the police department, was in Osaka that day. The police chief there, Kenji Tomita (later to become secretary-general of the Konoe Cabinet), was a disciple of Morihei, and he arranged for his teacher to be politely interrogated—albeit for over twelve hours—rather than imprisoned. When the Kyoto Police Department insisted on Morihei's detainment, Tomita had Morihei sent to Sonezaki, whose police chief hid Morihei in his own home until the storm blew over.

Morihei's supporters were able to protect him, mostly by convincing the prosecutors that he was too valuable an asset as a martial arts instructor to imprison, and many Omoto-kyo members bitterly resented the strings pulled on his behalf while so many others were thrown in jail. Onisaburo defended his ace bodyguard, perhaps hoping that Morihei could somehow secure his own release. (Ironically, in later years Morihei was idealized by the Omoto-kyo organization as a perfect example of the powers attainable through practice of the religion.)

The subsequent suppression of Omoto-kyo was one of the harshest in Japanese history. Everything of value at the Ayabe and Kameoka compounds was seized and auctioned off; 15,000 laborers were set to work dynamiting and torching every Omoto-kyo building; the remaining debris was bulldozed into the earth, and the property was sold. Anything remotely associated with Omoto-kyo was either burned, crushed, or tossed into the sea. Omoto-kyo leaders were tortured, and thousands of believers lost their jobs.

Onisaburo was imprisoned for more than six and a half years before finally being convicted of lese majesty—he was found innocent of inciting rebellion—in 1942. Then seventy-two years old and in poor health, no longer a threat to a government in the midst of waging a world war, Onisaburo was released on bond. In 1945 the new administration exonerated Onisaburo of all charges, and he was a free man. In a sense "resurrected," the irrepressible Onisaburo once more set out to build a Heaven on Earth; death, however, was the single obstacle that not even the Great Guru could overcome. The flamboyant religious leader succumbed at age seventy-eight, three years after the end of the war, and Omoto-kyo has never recovered from his loss—in fact, the organization has split into contending factions, with one group awaiting Onisaburo's imminent return to earth as a savior.

The authorities were not merely being paranoid about the threat of rebellion. A few years before the crackdown on Omoto-kyo, fanatic right-wingers and their sympathizers in the navy attempted to overthrow the civilian government and effect a Showa Restoration. The revolt was suppressed, but not before the assassination of the prime minister, Tsuyoshi Inukai. Three months after the Second Omoto-kyo Affair, on February 26, 1936, another coup was launched, this time by the "Imperial Way" faction of the army. Both Omoto-kyo and Morihei had links to some of the members responsible for these two revolts; it appears, however, that neither Onisaburo nor Morihei had direct knowledge of either plan.

In the chaos that followed, the political situation went from bad to worse. Japan initiated a war with China in 1937, bombed Pearl Harbor in 1941, and then suffered crushing defeat in 1945.

During these grim years Morihei was under tremendous strain. His beloved Guru and many of his Omoto-kyo friends were languishing in prison and Morihei himself was still under a cloud of suspicion for his Omoto-kyo ties and the involvement of several of his disciples in secret plots. It has been suggested that Morihei was allowed to escape prosecution in the Omoto-kyo incident as long as he continued teaching lethal techniques to the cadets at the Military Police Academy and the "espionage college" at Toyama. Although bayonet fighting and *judo* were on the curriculum, word quickly spread among the cadets that Morihei's Aiki-budo was the martial art to study because its techniques were the "most effective." Trainees at both places were, not unexpectedly, a bad lot of fellows, Gestapo-like characters who thought nothing of "ambushing" their instructor Morihei to test him. (Morihei, of course, escaped unharmed.)

On the other hand, many of the people directing the war effort were admirers of Morihei who frequently sought his counsel. These included the emperor, who was greatly impressed by Morihei's command performance, and two prime ministers: first, Fumimaro Konoe, one of the directors of the Kobukan, and then Prime Minister General Hideki Tojo, who was a keen student of Ueshiba-style *budo* when he was stationed in Manchuria.

For instance, Morihei was a highly influential figure in Manchukuo, the puppet empire established in 1932 by the Japanese army in northern China. Following a series of aborted covert missions, including Onisaburo's Mongolian Adventure, to establish a foothold in Manchuria and Inner Mongolia, the Japanese army acted overtly, eventually taking control of the entire area. In order to give the nation at least the appearance of independence, the last Ch'ing emperor, P'u-i, deposed when the republic was founded in 1912, was smuggled out of China—after much "encouragement" from the Japanese military—and installed as emperor.

Morihei was the chief martial arts instructor at the Kenkoku University established by the Japanese to train Japanese and Chinese officials to serve in the new government.

In fact, Aiki-budo was a required course for all the students at the university. The emperor P'u-i was an avid fan of Morihei's and once paid a visit to the *dojo* in Tokyo. Many of the senior officials in Manchuria were students of Morihei's.

It was during one of these trips to Manchuria that Morihei had his famous match with the *sumo* wrestler Tenryu. The controversial Tenryu had earlier failed in his attempt to reform the feudal world of professional Japanese *sumo* and had subsequently gone to Manchukuo to teach martial arts. At a demonstration by Morihei, Tenryu was urged by the crowd to challenge the sixty-year-old master. The huge Tenryu was totally unable to budge little Morihei, and then the heavyweight who had once bounced other behemoths on their ears found himself pinned to the floor with a single finger. Tenryu, thoroughly humbled, became one of Morihei's best pupils.

Morihei's prestige was so great that certain government officials secretly commissioned him to try to negotiate a peace settlement with the Chinese leaders; following Pearl Harbor, Japan was incapable of waging war on two fronts for very long. Nothing came of Morihei's efforts, however, and he suddenly retired from public life in 1942.

Why?

Morihei may have been a patriot, convinced that Japan was a divine country, but he was no fanatic willing to fight to the last man, woman, and child. He was acutely aware of the contradiction between discovering that *budo* was a Way of Love that fostered and preserved life and the massive death and destruction of war. Many of his later disciples recall his saying how much he detested teaching at the Military Police and Toyama academies, and he once complained to his son: "The military is dominated by reckless fools ignorant of statesmanship and religious ideals who slaughter innocent citizens indiscriminately and destroy everything in their path. They act in total contradiction to God's will, and they will surely come to a sorry end. True *budo* is to nourish life and foster peace, love, and respect, not to blast the world to pieces with weapons."

Also, after the attack on Pearl Harbor, Morihei quietly contacted knowledgeable acquaintances to learn all he could about Japan's adversary; he was told candidly by some that there was no hope of Japan's winning a prolonged conflict with that inexhaustibly rich nation.

Made physically and emotionally ill by the carnage, Morihei, pleading poor health and the desire to preserve the true way of Aiki at all costs, resigned all his positions, entrusted the operation of the *dojo* to his son and disciples, and moved to a farm in Iwama, about a hundred miles north of Tokyo. In his later years, Morihei intimated that his abrupt move to Iwama was at divine command. Morihei perceived that the "black rain" Nao Deguchi had prophesied would soon fall on Hiroshima and Nagasaki. An inner voice said to him, "Go to the country, build a shrine dedicated to the Great Spirit of Aiki, and prepare yourself to be a guiding light of a new Japan." (Morihei's timely

The buildings at the Aikido Shrine are very modest: a small Shinto gate (*tori-i*), little hall (*above*), and the tiny inner shrine (*left*). The buildings are merely the outer shell of an inner reality, a reality that each Aikido practitioner must seek within his or her own "living shrine."

resignation of his official duties also spared him the possibility of later being classified as a minor war criminal.) Interestingly, the term *Aikido* was formally adopted as the name of Morihei's art at about the same time.

Morihei never cared much for city life, and he had begun acquiring land in Iwama from around 1935 in hope of someday establishing a farm-*dojo* in the country. By the time of his retirement in 1942, Morihei's property had expanded to nearly seventeen acres, a sizable plot in cramped Japan. There were no buildings on the property, however, and Morihei bought a local farmer's shed and had it remodeled into a simple hut. Visitors from Tokyo were shocked to find Morihei and his wife, who had previously been literally and figuratively right in the middle of things before, living in such spartan accommodations. Morihei, on the contrary, was overjoyed to once again be in communion with the life-giving presence of Mother Nature.

During the rest of the war years, Morihei slowly recuperated—he was ill as long as his country was ill—and concentrated on constructing the Aiki Shrine. A *jinja,* or shrine, is an outer manifestation of an inner reality. Compared to the Grand Shrine at Ise and hundreds of other magnificent *jinja* in other parts of Japan, Morihei's little Aiki Jinja seems almost crude. The significance of that shrine lies not in the building itself but in the spirit contained within it.

Morihei's Aiki Shrine was dedicated to the forty-two guardian deities of the universe, each one personifying one of the elemental forces that sustain the cosmos—for example, energy, light, water, fire, and, of course, love—in other words, all the elements that activate and maintain the world. Ideally, one who approaches the Aiki Shrine becomes aware of the presence of such forces and, by extension, realizes what truly constitutes existence. The proper way to venerate the Aiki Jinja is to become one with the Great Spirit enshrined there and to embody it within oneself. This is what Morihei did every day and what he hoped his followers would also attempt.

The war reached its tragic conclusion on August 15, 1945, and Morihei, his health restored, was one of the few Japanese who were optimistic about the future. "Don't worry," he consoled his disheartened disciples. "Hereafter, the true Aikido will emerge."

4

THE INTRODUCTION OF AIKIDO TO THE WORLD got off to a slow start. Although the Tokyo *dojo* had survived the air raids intact owing to the heroic efforts of Morihei's son Kisshomaru, who doused all the flames threatening the training hall, thirty bombed-out neighborhood families, nearly one hundred people in all, squatted in the building. Even if the *dojo* had been usable, the U.S. Occupation authorities had banned the practice of all martial arts (with the exception of *karate*). A small *dojo* had been constructed on the Iwama property along with the Aiki Shrine, and Morihei, well out of view of the General Headquarters in Tokyo, trained quietly during the prohibition with a few of his battle-weary former disciples and some local youths.

In 1948 permission was granted by the Occupation authorities and the Japanese Ministry of Education to organize an Aiki Foundation to promote Aikido, "a martial way dedicated to the fostering of international peace and justice," and in 1949 the Tokyo *dojo* was officially reopened. (It took until 1955 to get the last of the squatters to leave.)

There were few new trainees at first. The public transportation system, destroyed during the war, was not yet completely rebuilt, and because of the severe food shortage people did not want to expend energy practicing the largely discredited martial arts. (One early trainee admitted that he became a live-in disciple simply because of the free meals he received.) As the economic situation improved, more trainees joined the *dojo*, and branches were gradually established all over Japan and at many universities. The first public demonstration was held in 1956. About the same time, foreigners began practicing Aikido seriously, and the art was spread overseas.

Morihei's second generation of students, those who entered during the war and in the early days of the Aikikai, included former Chief Instructor Koichi Tohei, who was a master of *ki* power but not as skilled in the *aiki* of human relations. Depending on whom one talks to, Tohei was either asked to leave or separated himself from the Headquarters Dojo after Morihei's death, subsequently creating his own organization. Minoru Hirai, Morihei's representative on the Butokukai, the Committee for the Martial Arts, during the war, also later opened his own school, called the Dai Nihon Korindo

Aikido. Another disciple who started his own organization is Kanshu Sunadomari of the Manseikan in Kyushu. Although Sunadomari is an Omoto-kyo believer and thus shares a similar outlook, his unique techniques, largely developed through individual experimentation, differ intriguingly from those of Morihei.

The two other disciples who are closest to Morihei in their religious views are Michio Hikitsuchi, a talented swordsman who is in charge of the Kumano Dojo, one of Morihei's favorite training halls, and calligrapher-Aikidoka Seiseki Abe, often referred to as "Morihei's best friend," who runs a small *dojo* in Osaka.

Several other senior disciples of Morihei's are still affiliated with the Headquarters Dojo. Zensaburo Ozawa, a disciple of the famous Soto Zen master Kodo Sawaki, sees Aikido as "moving Zen," executing the techniques with flawless precision and grace. Thoughtful Shigenobu Okumura, who followed the example of his mother and began training in Aikido in Manchuria, attracts a more intellectual type of student because of his learned presentations. Bansen Tanaka is the mainstay of Aikido in the Osaka area. Colorful Seigo Yamaguchi climbs Mount Fuji nearly every weekend during the summer, a classical example of religious devotion and physical training. Rough-and-tumble Sadateru Arikawa challenges his students to test themselves to the limit. Takuo Takaoka of Wakayama maintains the "old-style" of Aikido. Hardened veterans Morihiro Saito, head of the Iwama Dojo, and Hiroshi Isoyama, chief instructor of the Japan Defense Force, keep Aikido from degenerating into a form of light gymnastics. Innovative Shoji Nishio prefers training with a live blade. Hiroshi Tada, Nobuyoshi Tamura, and Kazuo Chiba spread the art overseas.

Compared with the drama and excitement of the previous years, Morihei's postwar career was relatively uneventful. He entrusted administrative details and popularization to his son Kisshomaru and the senior disciples, devoting all his time to further developing and refining his Way of Harmony.

In contrast to the restless, frenetic activity of his youth and middle age, Morihei's later years were characterized by a sense of peace and deep spirituality; he spent most of the time after the war praying, farming, and reading. He once wrote in an essay: "By secluding myself in Iwama and reducing my involvement with worldly affairs, I have been able to attain a deeper sense of oneness with the universe. I rise every morning at four, purify myself with *misogi* [cold-water ablutions], and then step outdoors to greet the rising sun. I link myself with the cosmos through *aiki* and commune with all things—I feel as if I am transformed into the universe itself, breathing in all phenomena. Standing before the altar of heaven and earth, I am in perfect harmony with the Divine. Then I bow in the four directions and pray and meditate before the Aiki Shrine for an hour and a half."

In his last years, Morihei did very little direct instructing, teaching instead by example and inspiration. He was a rather distant figure for most trainees, who only occa-

As Morihei grew older in the postwar years, the religious aspect of his character became increasingly prominent. Although there were occasional flashes of the old wrathful god (*left*), most of the photographs taken during his later years show him as a kindly old patriarch and wise philosopher. At right is a formal portrait dating from his mid-seventies.

Morihei at his leisure, relaxed yet ever-alert.

A reflective Morihei in front of the altar in the Iwama *dojo*.

sionally caught a glimpse of the phantom master. When he did lead the training, the emphasis was on the spiritual significance of Aikido; Morihei's lectures occupied at least half, if not more, of the practice session. He often told his disciples, "I am just a guide. Learn for yourselves."

One of the young trainees at Iwama related, "We high school students were always glad when the Founder [i.e., Morihei] conducted the training. He would spend twenty minutes or so performing *misogi-no-jo* and *chinkon-kishin*, talk for another twenty, demonstrate a few basic techniques, and then vanish. It was a welcome break from the regular bone-crunching practice sessions."

Morihei divided his time between Iwama and the Tokyo *dojo* with frequent instruction tours (until his eighties) to various parts of the country. In 1961 he made his first and only trip to the United States, a forty-day tour of Hawaii.

In the postwar period, Morihei did an about-face on the matter of public performances. Previously, he was adamantly opposed to open performances, lest his techniques be stolen by unsavory characters. He very reluctantly agreed to a public performance in 1956 after Kisshomaru pleaded with him to do so for the spread of Aikido; later, however, Morihei came to see the value of such demonstrations and let himself be freely photographed and filmed. (Except, on occasion, at Iwama. There were many *yakuza* in the town, and Morihei canceled several public demonstrations at the Aiki Shrine because of the presence of these gangsters.)

In fact, the first full-length feature film of Morihei was shot by an American television crew in 1958. Despite the crew's almost total lack of knowledge of Eastern thought, the hammy acting, a terrible demonstration by Koichi Tohei in which he was almost downed by a middle-aged, overweight novice, and an interview with Morihei in which he is obviously uncomfortable, this segment of the "Rendez-vous with Adventure" TV series still manages to convey the essence of Aikido. More dignified is the *King of Aikido* movie shot for Japanese television in 1961. It plays up the religious and mystical aspects of Aikido, portraying Morihei's daily training schedule in Iwama, often conducted late at night.

Morihei was showered with honors in his last years from both Japanese and foreign organizations, and he was especially pleased to be decorated by the emperor in 1964 at age eighty-one. (Kyuzo Mifune also received a medal at the same ceremony.)

A new three-story *dojo* was built in Tokyo in 1967 to handle the crush of new trainees; Morihei performed his final demonstration there on January 15, 1969.

Morihei collapsed on March 8 of the same year in Iwama. Aware that the end was near—"God is calling me"—Morihei rose early on the morning of March 10 to lead a

Morihei, terminally ill with liver cancer, giving his final public demonstration at the new Headquarters Dojo on January 15, 1969.

Close-up of Morihei taken in the last of his eighty-six years.

practice session for the last time. He was then hospitalized, his condition diagnosed as liver cancer. Morihei refused surgery and demanded to be returned home. There, as he awaited his final call, he smiled softly to himself each time he heard the sounds of practice arising from the *dojo* next door.

Even on his deathbed, Morihei was an invincible warrior. He went to the toilet unaided regardless of how ill he was. Just before his death, four of his disciples rushed to his assistance when he rose from the bed. Morihei instantly shrugged, and all four went flying out into the garden. On another such trip, he disappeared, and his disciples found him in the *dojo* teaching a bunch of children: "This is how you do it! This is how you do it!"

As Morihei's many disciples and friends called to bid farewell to their mentor, he told them, "Aikido is for the entire world. It is not for selfish or destructive purposes. Train unceasingly for the good of all."

Eighty-six-year-old Morihei "returned to the Source" early in the morning of April 26, 1969. One of his disciples who was present remarked, "Usually in cases of death by cancer, the face is contorted by pain, but Morihei's countenance was incredibly beautiful and serene. It was the face of a divine being."

For those who missed the opportunity to meet Morihei, he prophesied: "The world's chaos will worsen; expect my return."

Morihei with Onisaburo's daughter Naohi, currently head of Omoto-kyo. Throughout his life Morihei was a fervent believer in that eclectic creed.

5

NOW THAT THE DETAILS OF MORIHEI'S CAREER are known, let us look at the man himself.

Although Morihei's all-out drive to become first the strongest and then the most spiritual martial artist in the world resulted in the creation of the wonderful art of Aikido, his single-mindedness was hard on the people closest to him. Yoroku loved his only son more than anything in the world, but he could never figure the boy out. He gave Morihei everything he wanted and even attempted to follow his son to frigid Hokkaido—an excruciatingly difficult decision for one with roots in the sacred (and temperate) Kumano district. Yoroku may have been dismayed at Morihei's strange behavior but eventually resigned himself to the fact that his son was marching to a different drummer, as evidenced by his final words to Morihei: "Do what you really want."

Morihei's mother, like all Japanese women of that era, deferred to the men in her life, but even she opposed the move to Ayabe. (She died there in 1922 at age seventy-one.) It is regrettable that neither parent was around to witness Morihei's later success.

Morihei, at least in his early years, similarly ignored the feelings of his wife and children—in those days, it was up to the family to adjust to the father, not the other way around. It is clear from the writings of Kisshomaru that he resented his father's long absences from home and his unyielding stubbornness, typical of many men of the Meiji period. As noted above, Morihei at first did not think his skinny, bookworm son was up to succeeding him and therefore adopted Kiyoshi Nakakura. Morihei arranged the match without consulting with his daughter Matsuko, an old-fashioned custom, and it is not surprising that the union failed. (Two other disciples have claimed recently that Morihei had asked them to be his son-in-law, again without his daughter's apparent knowledge or consent.) While Morihei had real affection for his wife, that was an emotion a samurai never displayed or even acknowledged. In his last years, however, Morihei would joke lovingly when his formal kimono would get soiled in a demonstration, "The old lady will yell at me for this!" Hatsu died two months to the day after Morihei.

However admirable, Morihei's samurai disdain for money created endless troubles for his family. He exhausted his huge patrimony on the pursuit of his martial arts studies; he gave away several priceless swords to acquaintances who merely expressed their admiration for them; and he would refuse large, no-strings-attached donations if he happened to have enough money on hand at the time. Some of the wealthiest men in Japan were among his patrons, yet he never treated them any differently from the most impoverished live-in disciple. If a tycoon wished to make a contribution at an opportune time, fine; Morihei never requested money on his own. Any money received was placed on the Shinto altar. When operating funds were low, Mrs. Ueshiba was permitted to "borrow" the money from the gods. Except for a few really flush years during the heyday of the Kobukan, when Morihei's yearly income was over $100,000, the gods were frequently broke and Mrs. Ueshiba was forced to pass the word that immediate assistance was necessary. The disciples at Iwama, scolded by Morihei that he "was not teaching them for money," started a fund on their own to keep the buildings more or less in repair—a traditional *dojo* is expected to be somewhat run down, with nothing wasted on frivolous extras.

The heavy burden of raising money, running the *dojo,* and organizing the Aikikai fell on the shoulders of Kisshomaru, who, after all, was able to succeed his father as the Second-Generation Headmaster and place his own mark on the manner in which Aikido is interpreted and practiced.

For someone possessing superhuman strength, Morihei was in surprisingly delicate health much of his life. He suffered from constant stomach and liver disorders, caused in part, he maintained, by once engaging in a salt-water drinking contest with a Yoga practitioner when he was living in Ayabe. Morihei eschewed both meat and brown rice—even though Kenzo Futaki, "Dr. Brown Rice," was one of his prominent disciple-friends—preferring simple home-cooked meals and an occasional pick-me-up of chicken soup. Other than an infrequent sip of saké, Morihei neither drank nor smoked from his mid-fifties on. Perhaps many of his illnesses were psychosomatic, owing to his ultrasensitivity.

Although this ultrasensitivity made Morihei invulnerable to surprise attack, awake or asleep, it seriously complicated daily living. He could not board certain electric trains because the strong current of charged *ki* gave him unbearable headaches. Nor could he tolerate bathing in water used by others—a standard practice in Japan. If a disciple so much as lightly touched the surface of the water with his finger to test the temperature, Morihei could tell upon entering the bath and became furious. Similarly infuriated by a sudden burst of hot water from the shower in his hotel room, Morihei almost canceled his tour of Hawaii as soon as he got there. He was also bothered by the landing of insects on paper doors and restless trainees who lay awake in their beds several doors distant.

Every year on April 29, a memorial service is held for Morihei at the Aiki Shrine. Here Morihei's son and successor, Kisshomaru, gives a commemorative demonstration on one such occasion.

When traveling, Morihei insisted on being at the train station hours before departure, and if he sensed the slightest trace of "negative *ki*" anywhere along the line, he refused to budge. Often something would arouse his suspicion en route; thereupon he would announce, "I'm getting off," leap up, disembark at the next station, and take a return train home, regardless of how large a welcoming party was awaiting his arrival at the other end.

Occasionally, Morihei's ultrasensitivity was useful. During a stay in Osaka, Morihei received word that his wife was seriously ill. He planned to return to Tokyo on the first train in the morning, but suddenly in the middle of the night he woke up and told his disciple to cancel the trip because the danger had passed. A telegram arrived later bearing the news that Mrs. Ueshiba had recovered her health.

Morihei sorely tested the mettle of the disciples who accompanied him on these journeys. The heavily laden bag-carrier had to buy the tickets, get them punched, and try never to take his eye off the speedy Morihei, who did his best to lose his attendant—a sort of catch-me-if-you-can martial arts game. (Morihei never bumped into people, no matter how large the crowd, making it especially difficult for less agile trainees to catch up with him.) Once in a while, Morihei would give both his accompanying disciple and the welcoming party the slip and hop into a taxi, demanding that the bewildered driver take him to the "Aikido demonstration" without giving him the place or address, which Morihei did not know. On shorter streetcar rides Morihei would catch falling packages when the car made a sudden stop, berating his disciples for not doing likewise because of inattention. One day the streetcar Morihei was riding on collided with another vehicle. At the instant of impact, Morihei shouted, and the car flipped over and landed upright without injury to any of the passengers.

In spite of the great strain of being Morihei's attendant, disciples clamored for the honor of accompanying their master; all agree that the experience—carrying his heavy bags, massaging his legs during the trip, preparing a bath of just the right temperature, sleeping outside the door of his room in order to lead the way to the toilet when he rose at night, and seeing him safely back home—was the supreme test. A disciple could count on losing ten to fifteen pounds during a journey, and one disciple joked that his weight fell as soon as he heard Morihei would be coming.

Morihei's dreadful temper was legendary. Part of the phenomenon was cultural: Japanese teachers in general and martial arts instructors in particular are expected to be on a short fuse, ever ready to explode over some minor infraction or impropriety, thus keeping their charges perpetually on their toes. When Morihei was set off, his roars of disapproval sent everyone fleeing for cover.

Once in the 1930s when bread was a rarity in Japan, a disciple acquired a loaf for Morihei. Morihei instructed the disciple to eat it himself since he, Morihei, had a bad stomach. The hungry disciple called the others to share the treat but then discovered

The dignified Morihei never carried money or train tickets when on a journey, leaving all that up to his attendants. Overawed by his majestic appearance, ticket takers were too timid to stop Morihei at the gate when he entered before his accompanying disciple could catch up.

that the bread had gone moldy. They discarded it, uneaten, in a refuse bin, where Morihei accidentally saw it. "How dare you throw away a present from your master!" Morihei thundered. When told that the bread was moldy, Morihei raged, "*What!* Offering spoiled food to your teacher!" The walls of the Kobukan rattled with Morihei's anger. After the outburst, Morihei's normal disposition returned. "Don't worry," he said, smiling at his terrified disciples, "it was only the wrathful gods that were displeased with you. Everything is all right now!"

A live-in disciple in Iwama once made the mistake of buying the same kind of Japanese *geta* shoes as Morihei and, sure enough, one day the master slipped into them by mistake.

"Excuse me, O-sensei," the disciple meekly said, "those are my *geta*. Yours are over here."

"Idiot!" Morihei shouted. "Why did you get a pair similar to your teacher's!"

The disciple cleverly took out his fountain pen and covered his *geta* with ink. "They are different now."

One day at the Tokyo *dojo,* a middle-school student trainee who had never been told about Morihei saw the eighty-year-old teacher performing some techniques. As Morihei left the *dojo,* the teenager cracked, "Hi, Pops. What's an old geezer like you

63

doing here?" Morihei hit the ceiling, his fury not directed at the boy, who did not know any better, but at his instructors, who had not taught all the trainees about the Founder of Aikido.

A final word on the various names Morihei employed during his career. His given name was Morihei, "Abundant Peace." After the Mongolian Adventure, he adopted his Chinese name, pronounced *Moritaka* in Japanese; it means "Protector of the High." He very briefly used the penname Seigan, "True Vision," when the Kobukan was first opened, and then Tsunemori, "Eternal Abundance," under the influence of *kotodama* theory. In his last years, however, he returned to his original name: "I came into this world a Morihei and wish to go out of it a Morihei."

PART TWO

The Martial Artist

Do not look upon this world with fear and loathing.
Bravely face whatever the gods offer.
—MORIHEI UESHIBA

I

MORIHEI WAS UNDOUBTEDLY the greatest martial artist who ever lived. Even if we accept every exploit of all the legendary warriors, East and West, as being literally true, none of those accomplishments can be compared to Morihei's documented ability to disarm any attacker, throw a dozen men simultaneously, and down and pin opponents without touching them, recorded scores of times in photographs, on film, and by personal testimony.

How did Morihei become invincible?

One factor was his vast practical and theoretical knowledge of Eastern and Western martial arts. Like Aizu-Wakamatsu in Fukushima, Morihei's birthplace, Tanabe, was a "treasury of the martial arts," with one important difference; the influence of the Shinto cult of Kumano was so pervasive that the martial traditions originating in Wakayama always had a more spiritual cast than the win-at-any-cost methods of the Aizu fighters.

In his youth Morihei learned of the Aioi Ryu (probably an offshoot of the Sekiguchi Ryu) from the stories told about his grandfather, a famous exponent of the art. This and related systems stressed the importance of freely applying the "hard" and the "soft" according to each particular situation.

Morihei's first real training in the martial arts began with *sumo*, traditional Japanese wrestling. It was due to the head-on collisions common in *sumo* that Morihei started to toughen his skull by pounding it against a pole or stone hundreds of times each day. Since *sumo* requires powerful hips and legs, the young Morihei did a lot of jogging in the heavy sand and shallow water along the seashore to build those muscles. Another requirement of *sumo* is good balance; one must not let any part of the body (except of course for the feet) touch the ground. This precludes "sacrifice throws" in which one goes down first, hoping that one's momentum will carry the opponent over and down. One must overpower the opponent to win. While there is certainly an element of flexibility in *sumo*—even 400-pound mountains of flesh must be able to touch their foreheads to the ground with their legs stretched straight out—in general the emphasis is on the hard elements of pushing, thrusting, and lifting.

In Tanabe, Morihei also learned to wield a harpoon with deadly accuracy, a skill that demands a sharp eye, strong arms, and perfect balance even on a rocking boat.

It is unclear exactly how much Morihei practiced during his brief sojourn in Tokyo as a teenager. He apparently visited several *dojo*s and trained a bit at the places mentioned in Part One, but because of his preoccupation with getting his business started and his poor physical condition (beri-beri), Morihei did not make much progress.

Following his induction into the Imperial Army, Morihei received instruction in the use of firearms and the basics of Western military science. He continued to excel at *sumo* and also became highly proficient in the do-or-die combat art of bayonet fighting. In those days military encounters still involved hand-to-hand fighting, and in actual combat a soldier could not afford to let an enemy score a single point against his body. Other than an explosive thrust, there are no techniques in bayonet fighting; consequently, everything depends on timing—or "anticipation," as it is called in the Japanese martial arts. One must either instantly perceive an opponent's window of vulnerability and move in decisively or else immediately evade and counter an attack by "opening" to one side or the other.

The importance of Morihei's early training in *sumo* and bayonet fighting and their respective emphasis on keeping one's center of gravity low and entering directly (*irimi*) should not be overlooked.

Morihei's first systematic training in the classical Japanese martial arts began around the same time as his induction into the service. He enrolled in the *dojo* of Masakatsu Nakai, master teacher of Goto Ryu Yagyu Jujutsu. This *ryu* (school) originated in the body techniques employed by the illustrious Yagyu family of warriors; it was modified by several different masters over the centuries and then formed into a composite system in the nineteenth century. In Yagyu martial art systems, mind plays just as important a role as technique. In fact, mental power—an unperturbed, immovable mind—will always prevail over brute strength. A famous anecdote, told to every Yagyu trainee, goes like this:

Iemitsu, the third Tokugawa shogun, received a tiger as a gift from the Korean court. Iemitsu challenged the famous Shinkage Ryu swordsman Yagyu Tajima Munenori to subdue the beast. Yagyu immediately accepted the challenge and strode confidently into the cage. Just as the beast was about to pounce, he thumped the snarling animal on the head with his iron fan. The tiger shrank back and cowered in a corner. The Zen monk Takuan, who happened to be present, chided Yagyu, "That is the wrong approach." Takuan then entered the cage unarmed. When the tiger reared to attack, Takuan spat on his hands and gently rubbed the tiger's face and ears. The ferocious animal calmed down at once, purring and rubbing itself against the monk. "That's how you do it!" Takuan exclaimed.

Nakai was highly regarded for both his skill at the martial arts and his noble character. There is a tale that once during an early open *jujutsu* competition in Osaka, one of Nakai's disciples defeated a top Kokodan *judo* man. Upset by the loss, Jigoro Kano, then still a hot-tempered young man, issued a challenge to Nakai's senior disciple. Nakai severely scolded Kano for such intemperate behavior: it is improper for a master instructor to engage a lower-ranked trainee merely because he happened to defeat a disciple. Both the teacher and the disciple must reflect on the reason for the defeat and then apply for a rematch when they feel that they are ready.

Since Nakai was additionally proficient in sword, spear, and *jo* techniques, it is likely that Morihei trained in those arts during his four and a half years of apprenticeship. Morihei received a Goto Ryu Yagyu Jujutsu teaching license from Nakai in 1908 at age twenty-five. Even though Morihei studied a number of different systems, this is the only full teaching license he obtained.

After his son's discharge from the army, Yoroku built a *dojo* for Morihei; Morihei instructed there as well as sponsoring the visits of famous *jujutsu* and *judo* teachers.

After acquiring formidable physical and mental strength, Morihei found himself in Hokkaido, where he was initiated into the mysteries of *aiki* by Sokaku Takeda of the Daito Ryu.

While many traditional elements were absorbed into the system, it must be stated categorically that the Daito Ryu was the creation of one man and one man only, Sokaku Takeda. The core techniques that Sokaku inherited from Tanomo are said to have originated with Minamoto (Genji) Yoshimitsu around A.D. 1100. Yoshimitsu's son moved to Koga and established the Takeda clan; the art was secretly transmitted among family members from generation to generation. In 1754 the Takeda clan shifted its base of operations to Aizu-Wakamatsu, and there the system, known as *oshiki-uchi* or *odome,* was taught to high-ranking samurai men and women.

As noted previously, these techniques were passed along to Saigo Tanomo, who combined the highly effective blows, locks, pins, and throws of *oshiki-uchi* with the harmonization and breath control methods of *aiki-inyo.* This unified system was taught to Sokaku, who in turn added other elements based on his extensive firsthand experience in combat. For instance, Sokaku learned from his big battle with the construction gang that the regular *seigan* stance (with sword held horizontally) was ineffective when confronted by a swarm of attackers. The *jodan* stance (with sword held over one's head) was far superior, facilitating lightning-fast counters, and Sokaku incorporated such knowledge into his teaching.

The Japanese martial arts world is extremely conservative, and anyone presumptuous enough to create a new school was immediately hit with a barrage of criticism. To avoid trouble, Sokaku, who initially called his system the Yamato Ryu, decided to change it to Daito Ryu and had formal documents drawn up tracing the lineage back to Yoshimitsu. Daito was the name of Yoshimitsu's mansion and further referred to the Daito (Great East) Prosperity Sphere then being promoted by Japanese imperialists. Sokaku thereafter styled himself thirty-fifth Grandmaster of the Daito Ryu.

(Quite similarly to Morihei, Sokaku continually modified his techniques over the years, and there are distinct differences in the way his early and later disciples execute them. These discrepancies have resulted in several schisms within the Daito Ryu, the most serious breach being between Sokaku's son Tokimune and Sokaku's one-time designated successor Yukiyoshi Sagawa.)

At any rate, the thirty-two-year-old Morihei was easily defeated, for the first and only time in his life, by a skinny gnome twenty-five years his senior. Sokaku told Morihei, "If there is any reserve or hesitation, even a skilled practitioner can be easily defeated. Hear the soundless sound, see the formless form. At a glance, control your opponent and attain victory without contention. This is the inner meaning of *aiki*."

In Hokkaido, Morihei was initially given instruction in the "108 Basic Techniques" of Sokaku's Daito Ryu. Many of these techniques—for example, *shiho-nage, chokusen irimi nage, ikkyo* through *gokyo, suwari waza,* and *hanmi-hantachi*—are still practiced, in greatly altered form, in present-day Aikido and may be considered the roots of certain Aikido movements. However, there are many other movements that have nothing to do with the Daito Ryu.

Sokaku opened Morihei's eyes to the potential power of *aiki* timing, breath control, and the unity of body, sword, and stick techniques. Nevertheless, Morihei learned very little from Sokaku following the first period in Hokkaido, and in fact complained to confidants that Sokaku showed him nothing new during later visits to Ayabe and Tokyo. On his part, Morihei pursued his own independent studies of different traditions. In short, the influence of Sokaku's Daito Ryu on the development of Aikido should not be overemphasized. As Morihei clearly stated, "The direct influence of Sokaku's Daito Ryu techniques on the formation of Aikido is not that great. It was but one element among many."

What are some of the other martial arts Morihei studied?

Around age forty-two Morihei seems to have secluded himself in the mountains of Kumano and practiced Kuki Shin Ryu, a secretly transmitted martial art devised by mountain ascetics (*yamabushi*). Many of Morihei's *jo* techniques evidently originated from this *ryu* because the chief weapon of the ascetics was their staff/walking stick, which they carried with them at all times.

Incidentally, the Kuki Shin Ryu is closely associated with several of the modern *ninjutsu* schools. In the early days, Morihei occasionally demonstrated *ninja* techniques, as in the following anecdote:

His disciples asked Morihei if the feats attributed to *ninja* were really true. "You have been watching too many movies," Morihei said. "Grab your swords and sticks, and I'll give you a real demonstration of *ninjutsu* right out in the open." Ten or so disciples surrounded Morihei in the center of the *dojo* and attacked simultaneously; they felt a stream of air as Morihei disappeared and then heard him calling to them halfway up a staircase twenty feet away. When they requested another feat, Morihei yelled, "Are you trying to kill me just to entertain yourselves? Each time one performs such techniques, his life span is reduced by five to ten years."

Ninjutsu is the antithesis of Aikido. It is an art based on stealth, deception, and dirty tricks; yet even with their reliance on the vaunted "techniques of invisibility" and an arsenal of exotic weapons, none of the famous *ninja* of the past could have stood a chance against the divine techniques of Morihei, formulated in accordance with the principles of love and harmony.

Among other disciplines that Morihei investigated were the Take-no-uchi and Kito Jujutsu Ryus, Hozoin Ryu spear fighting, and several schools of swordsmanship, notably the Yagyu Ryu and the Katori Shinto Ryu. At Ayabe, Morihei concentrated on Hozoin Ryu spear techniques, hanging sponge balls in the trees all around him and then spearing them as accurately and as quickly as possible for hours and hours. Morihei had a close relationship with the Yagyu Ryu swordsman Kosaburo Shomojo for many years; despite variations, Morihei's basic sword stance and pair techniques were those of the Yagyu Ryu.

Because of his extensive travels in China, Morihei had wide exposure to that nation's martial arts traditions; somewhat surprisingly, he seems not to have taken much interest in them, not even *t'ai-chi*, which appears to have the most in common with Aikido. Since there were no Chinese masters on the same level as Morihei, he likely dismissed, perhaps unjustly, mainland martial arts as unworthy of serious study.

Morihei had an incredible ability to assimilate martial arts techniques. One day a famous classical Japanese dance teacher visited the Kobukan to request instruction in the halberd (*naginata*). Morihei hesitated a bit because he had little experience with that particular weapon, which was mainly used by females. Charmed, however, by the lovely teacher, he consented. Morihei ordered a disciple to obtain a popular novel in which the hero is a master of *naginata*, place the book on the Shinto altar, and see that he not be disturbed for the remainder of the day.

When the dance instructor returned for her lesson, Morihei showed her a series of beautiful moves. Later, after the woman had performed them on stage, she was told by a surprised *naginata* master, "What wonderful techniques! Where did you learn them?"

His puzzled disciples asked Morihei how he was able to master the *naginata* so quickly.

"The hero of the novel visited me while I was in a trance and taught me his secrets" was the reply—Morihei's fanciful way of saying that the universally applicable principles of *aiki* enabled him to formulate techniques freely with any type of weapon. Similarly, when Morihei had his disciples read popular novels to him, upon hearing the famous battle scenes described, Morihei would leap up and act out the heroes' movements.

Although Morihei absorbed an enormous number of martial arts techniques from diverse sources, it is incorrect to think of Aikido as derivative of the older traditions. Aikido, Morihei insisted, is a totally new and revolutionary system, independently created with a special set of principles and ideals.

Morihei's genius for the martial arts was coupled with extraordinary physical strength and stamina. In Hokkaido, Morihei built up his already formidable power through heavy farm work with specially weighted tools, wrestling with huge logs, and long-distance running. Even in his fifties, Morihei seemed nearly as wide as he was tall. "Scrubbing his back during a bath," an early disciple recalls, "was like polishing stone. His stomach muscles were so thick that they formed a triangle." Morihei's grip was crushing, leaving bruise marks for days on the spots he had held or merely touched. Once Morihei inadvertently broke the wrist of a *karate* master by lightly blocking a punch with his fingers.

Tales of his unbelievable ability to move boulders and lift logs abound. Once, in Takeda, his disciple Yukawa, whose nickname was Samson, was furiously attempting to uproot a small tree. "Too much strain! Too much strain!" Morihei laughed as he grabbed the five-inch-diameter tree and yanked it cleanly from the earth.

Morihei retained his muscle tone well into his seventies and in Iwama did twice as much farm work twice as fast as the teenage trainees. In purely physical terms, Morihei was one of the strongest men ever to tread this earth.

In addition to his fantastic muscular strength, Morihei discovered how to plug into the unlimited current of breath (*kokyu*) and *ki* power that circulates through the universe. Put in the simplest possible terms, *kokyu*, the Japanese equivalent of the Sanskrit *prana*, is the vital breath of life, and *ki* is the waves of energy that emanate from *kokyu*. Every Japanese art underscores the importance of fostering breath and *ki* power. One's *kiai*, a forceful inner and outer projection of *kokyu* and *ki* power, indicates the level of one's coordination of body and mind. *Kiai* is usually thought of as merely the shout emitted at the instant a technique is executed. For most trainees, this is true, but for advanced practitioners a *kiai* is a perfectly concentrated burst of energy, only part of which is audible.

Morihei's *kiai* was, not surprisingly, irresistible. "Use your *kiai* as a weapon," he instructed his disciples. His could be heard more than half a mile away; even when he was not shouting out loud, he projected terrific waves. Once, during a service at a Buddhist temple, Morihei joined the congregation in the recitation of the *Heart Sutra*. Although Morihei was chanting at the same level as the others in the group, the priest felt as if the sounds rising from Morihei were solidly pounding him on the back.

On another occasion, Morihei was demonstrating before the president of a large newspaper company, when the president thought to himself, "This is all fake." At that instant, Morihei let loose with an explosive *kiai,* and all the flashbulbs in the cameras of the news photographers went flying out of their sockets.

Morihei was often photographed and filmed having a bunch of men pushing against him with all their might without being able to budge the suddenly immovable fixture. Morihei could even perform the feat with a stick held out horizontally from his body while five or six men attempted to force it sideways; Morihei kept them at bay and then flipped them down with a slight twist of his wrist. Several of Japan's top baseball players became Morihei's students after swinging their bats full force against Morihei's sword; instead of knocking the sword from Morihei's hands, the proud athletes were stunned to have their bats driven back in their own direction.

In these cases, Morihei was subtly attuned to the others' outflow of *ki* and could imperceptibly counter it with a stronger flow of his own. Morihei devised a series of *kokyu-ho* techniques to help his disciples develop breath and *ki* power. Some, like the "unbendable arm," can be learned by anyone in a few minutes; others, like throwing one's opponent without touching him or her, require a lifetime of training.

Extensive training, physical strength, and breath and *ki* power are still not enough; to be really invincible one needs an uncanny sixth sense.

For years and years, Morihei's disciples tried to catch him off guard—Morihei promised a teaching license to anyone who could do so—but even at night there was some part of the master that was ever awake: "Who is that trying to sneak up on me?" Morihei revealed that beams of energy continually radiated from his body and that as soon as a hostile force entered that field, he was instantly alerted.

Once a disciple who noticed that Morihei always evaded to the right when he attacked him with a straight blow dared to cross up his teacher by immediately striking in that direction. Morihei stood right where he was in front of the startled swordsman: "What on earth are you doing?"

Another time, a young disciple facing Morihei with a sword thought of launching a sneak attack; Morihei's eyes opened wide with a frightful glare, and that was the end of that. At a celebration, several disciples wondered among themselves if Morihei would be vulnerable after drinking saké; Morihei, on the other side of the room, whirled around and scowled at them.

A noted *karate* instructor became Morihei's pupil after visiting the *dojo* and being told nonchalantly by the Aikido master, "Strike me if you can!" So saying, Morihei turned his back on the expert, who swung away without coming close to the elusive elf.

As soon as Morihei entered a *dojo,* he immediately paid his respects to the Shinto altar. After doing so during a visit to a *dojo* of one of his disciples, he called the instructor over and berated him: "Why did you neglect to chant the morning service today? The *kamisama* is lonely!"

Once a sculptor was commissioned to do a bust of Morihei's muscular upper torso.

When it was finished, Morihei checked the rear of the bust and said, "This muscle and this muscle are not quite right." Upon closer examination, the sculptor was shocked to find it so. Morihei knew exactly how his back looked even though he couldn't see it!

Typically, Morihei attributed his sixth sense to divine protection. A disciple accompanying Morihei on a trip, noticing that Morihei had closed his eyes to nap, thought, "Now is my chance!" The elated disciple reached for his fan to strike Morihei on the head. Morihei's eyes shot open.

"My guardian deity tells me that you are thinking of hitting me over the head. You wouldn't do such a thing, would you?"

Whatever the source, all of the great martial artists developed a similar sixth sense, perhaps acquired from the decades of peering into the inner reaches of the human heart and having a mind set forever in the training hall.

2

MORIHEI CEASELESSLY REFINED HIS UNIQUE ART; consequently, Aikido underwent numerous permutations during the Founder's forty-year teaching career.

The signboard at Morihei's first *dojo* in Ayabe read *Daito Ryu Aikijutsu,* but following his move to Tokyo and the subsequent founding of the Wakamatsu Dojo, his system was known as, among other things, Kobukan Aiki-Budo, Ueshiba Ryu Jujutsu, Tenshin Aiki-Budo, and finally, from 1942, Aikido.

The Aiki-Budo of the period 1932–1942 was rigorous, direct, and practical. In this decade, Morihei's tremendous physical power and technical prowess were the dominant elements; it was hard-style, aggressive *budo* characterized by razor-sharp execution of the techniques and muscular strength. A spiritual element was always present in Morihei's presentation of the art, but because his disciples repeatedly faced challengers and because the country was preparing for and then engaged in war, the techniques had to be 100 percent effective. Extensive use was made of devastating blows to anatomical weak points (*atemi*); throws were carried out with full extension to bring an opponent down and out, and pins were applied with joint-wrenching and bone-crunching force. Weapons study centered on the combat arts of spear, bayonet, and sword fighting.

An early disciple relates: "People hesitated to challenge Morihei because of his reputation, but we assistant instructors were continually put to the test by *judo* men, *kendo* men, *sumo* wrestlers, boxers, and just plain street fighters. We always attempted to avoid such confrontations, but usually there was no alternative. And once the contest commenced, there is no way we would allow ourselves to be defeated."

Two instruction manuals and one film were produced under Morihei's supervision during the Aiki-Budo years. (A series of techniques was photographed in the Noma Dojo in 1936 but never made public; Morihei also had a hand in the compilation of a textbook on arrest techniques for the Military Police Academy.)

Budo renshu appeared in 1933. The pictures were drawn by Miss Kunagoshi with several of the live-in disciples posing as models. Morihei evidently intended the book to be a kind of license presented to advanced students: "Read this book, train diligently,

75

Two shots taken during Morihei's classic Aiki-Budo years. (*Top*) Solidly based with *ki* power flowing through his extended fingertips, Morihei has broken his opponent's posture and holds him suspended, unable to respond. (*Bottom*) Although in actual combat one would never allow an opponent to get behind oneself, Morihei advocated the practice of rear techniques to foster awareness of attacks one cannot directly see—one must adjust to the feel of the opponent and not his appearance. Here Morihei has swept the opponent off his feet and onto Morihei's hips, where he can be easily thrown.

and that will enable you to be enlightened to the inner principles of the martial arts and become a true master."

The manual opens with a collection of Morihei's *doka* ("songs of the way"). These are didactic poems, written in the 5-7-5-7-7-syllable *waka* form, by masters to inspire and instruct their disciples. *Doka* rarely have much literary merit, and Morihei's were no exception; their primary purpose is to reveal the essence of an art in a few pithy phrases. Morihei's *doka* run from the commonsensical:

> *One who is*
> *well prepared*
> *for anything that arises*
> *will never rashly draw*
> *his sword in haste.*

> *Progress*
> *comes to those*
> *who train and train;*
> *reliance on secret techniques*
> *will get you nowhere.*

to the practical:

> *If the enemy assumes*
> *a lower stance,*
> *remain in the middle stance*
> *unwavering,*
> *immovable.*

> *When an enemy*
> *rushes in*
> *to strike,*
> *step to the side*
> *and cut him down instantly.*

to the mysterious:

> *Penetrate reality*
> *by mastering the*
> kiai *YAH!*

*Do not be deceived
by the enemy's ploys.*

*The active and passive
spirits perfectly harmonized,
forming the cross of* aiki;
*advance ever onward,
pouring out manly vigor.*

The short text is a similar jumble of the plain, the practical, and the esoteric. In spite of all the material published under his name, Morihei had absolutely no literary ability—his multifaceted mind precluded him from collecting his thoughts into coherent sentences. It was his disciples and scholarly friends who edited his words into more or less comprehensible form. (I have taken similar liberties; all of the quotes that appear in this book were culled from the huge corpus of oral and written literature.)

The most interesting statements in the text, no doubt directed toward his many followers in the military, are these:

The true martial art is the one that defeats an enemy without sacrificing a single man; attain victory by placing yourself always in a safe and unassailable position.

True *budo* is for the sake of peace and harmony; train daily to manifest this spirit throughout the world.

Since the illustrations in *Budo renshu* were roughly sketched, they are difficult to follow; in 1938 *Budo*, professionally photographed with Morihei himself posing for the pictures, was typeset and privately circulated. The manual opens with these words: "Budo is a divine path formulated by the gods, the basis of the true, the good, and the beautiful; it reflects the absolute and unlimited inner workings of the universe. The virtue acquired through assiduous training enables one to perceive the essential principles of Heaven and Earth." Morihei goes on to say, "Purify the body and mind, link yourself to the Divine, manifest the hidden, and strive for enlightenment." In addition to the standard body techniques—*tai-no-henko, irimi nage, shiho-nage, kotegaeshi, ikkyo* through *gokyo,* and *kokyu-ho*—this manual includes sword, spear, and bayonet techniques. It also includes the warning "This manual is not to be shown to non-Japanese."

By far the most interesting relic of the Aiki-Budo era is a film shot in Osaka in 1935 when Morihei was fifty-two years old. Morihei, then at his physical peak, is shown whirling around the *dojo,* throwing his disciples halfway across the room, pinning them with precise holds, and deftly dealing with armed attacks. At first, Morihei appears to

78

be merely a supremely skilled technician and strong man; it is not until the end of the film, when he is grabbed full strength by ten men, that viewers realize that they are witnessing something inexplicable. Morihei emits a peculiar *kiai,* and they all fly off him and hit the mat.

While the core techniques remained essentially the same, Morihei's techniques, reflecting changes in his philosophy, became softer and more circular in postwar Aikido. He now maintained that if one has the power to walk, it is possible to practice Aikido. One man wanted to learn Aikido more than anything but was advised not to do so by his doctor. The man had been very ill as a youth, spending years in and out of hospitals, and was extremely weak physically. Morihei went out of his way to teach the man simple warm-up exercises and then later to engage him in sword partner practice. After the student built up some strength in his arms and legs, Morihei had him practice seated techniques. The man persevered, eventually becoming an instructor. Other young trainees were assigned to massage duty, working on Morihei's legs and shoulders to strengthen their wrists for Aikido training.

Morihei's gradual ascent into the highest realms of pure *ki* and *kokyu* power had a deleterious effect on some of his later followers. In his final public demonstration, the phantomlike Morihei downed his partners by simply waving his hand or pointing his finger at them. Morihei, of course, had reached such a fluid stage after sixty years of solid training. Unfortunately, many modern practitioners favor this "no touch" approach, throwing each other about with a flick of the wrist or a cockeyed, off-balance toss of the shoulder. If your partner is going to fall down anyway, why worry about proper distancing, lack of vulnerability, or concentrated power?

Morihei's mind was forever in the training hall, and each minute of the day was a time for him to practice, but he also engaged in special sessions. In the prewar period these would take place on Mount Kurama, near Kyoto. Morihei would take two or three disciples with him for a twenty-one-day training session. The small group lived on rice, pickles, miso soup, and wild herbs. Morihei would rise at 5:00 A.M. to pray. After morning prayers and *misogi,* they would swing heavy swords 500 times and then practice footwork. From ten o'clock to noon they trained in body techniques. Afternoon training ran from three to five; the disciples took turns acting as Morihei's partner as he ran through series after series of techniques. In the evening the disciples would review the day's training.

Every three days, Morihei would announce at midnight, "Time for night training." The disciples could discern nothing in the pitch-darkness, but Morihei cried out to them, "Watch out for the rock on your left! Duck to avoid the upcoming branches!" He armed them with wooden swords and commanded them to attack. At first, none of the disciples had the slightest notion where their teacher was; gradually, however, they sensed his presence to the right or left and speeded up their attacks. Then Morihei turned the tables: he chased after them, bringing his razor-sharp blade within a hair's-breadth of their headbands. (Incidentally, many famous Japanese warriors engaged in ascetic training on Mount Kurama over the centuries; the *tengu* said to be residing there was a master of military science.)

In the postwar years, similar sessions took place at Atago Mountain near Iwama and in Tokyo at the ruins of Toyama Military Academy, site of one of Morihei's old haunts. Morihei was devoted to training in the dead of night, in the light of the full moon, thrusting and thrusting against a tree, pounding and pounding a heavy wooden sword against a stack of thick branches. (Morihei would not allow the use of lanterns or flashlights at night: "Samurai have to learn how to see in the dark!" He also scolded his disciples for walking on his right side, blocking his controlling hand: "Keep on the left where you can be protected.")

Morihei's instruction was not systematic. He insisted, "Aikido has no techniques." That is, the movements are rooted in natural principles, not abstract or rigid formulas. He would explain such-and-such a movement as a function of such-and-such a deity or divine principle, demonstrate it, and have his trainees attempt it. Questions were discouraged—if there was a problem, Morihei would show the technique once more, saying, "See what I mean?" Occasionally he gave cryptic hints such as "Surge forward from the Great Earth" or "Billow like the Great Waves" and "Use One to Strike All!"; but in general the basic principle was "Learn and forget! Learn and forget! Make the techniques part of your being!"

Proficiency is acquired only through long and diligent training; overly detailed explanations and excessive rationalization of the movements simply serve to confuse and eventually trivialize what is divinely inspired. That is why Morihei said, "An instructor shows only a very small part of Aikido. Through ceaseless, diligent training, discover the ramifications of each technique, slowly, one by one, instead of piling up technique after technique."

In his later years, especially when he was sequestered in Iwama, Morihei tended to run through techniques in a series of related movements and emphasized the sword and *jo*. On the other hand, he would show up unannounced at the Tokyo *dojo*, demonstrate a whirlwind of techniques, and then dash out. A disciple once said to him, "When you are in the *dojo* I can perform the techniques perfectly, but when you leave I cannot recall a thing." Morihei replied, "That is because I link your *ki* with mine and invisibly guide you. If you are ever in doubt or in trouble, just think of me and I will assist you."

Morihei studied many kinds of weapons over the years but ultimately settled on the sword and the *jo* as his "instruments of purification."

In *Budo* Morihei stated: "The sword of *aiki*, in which Heaven, Earth, and human beings are harmonized, empowers one to cut through and destroy all evil, thereby restoring this beautiful world to its innate purity." A *doka* from this manual goes:

The penetrating brilliance of a sword
wielded by a man of the Way
strikes at the enemy
lurking deep within
one's own body and mind.

In *Takemusu Aiki,* a collection of Morihei's postwar talks, he related this tale:

> One night, as I was swinging my sword in my garden, I was suddenly confronted by an apparition armed with a sword. At first I could do nothing against him, but gradually I began parrying his lightning-fast attacks. The apparition returned the following two evenings and then vanished. Thereafter, whenever I held a sword, I lost all sense of sword, opponent, time, and space; I was breathing in the universe—no, the universe was contained within me. One swing of the sword gathers up all the mysteries of the cosmos.

Morihei's swordsmanship was so free-form that it raised criticism in some quarters for being too unorthodox; in truth, however, Morihei's sword was the real *kendo*—he unfailingly assumed the appropriate stance and reacted naturally to any attack.

In his last years, Morihei employed the *jo* as an instrument of purification in the divine dance he performed before training to calm his spirit and cleanse the *dojo. Misogi-no-jo* is a heartfelt prayer for peace and harmony expressed through the medium of the staff and body movements.

Everyone agrees that Morihei was a different person in the training hall. He seemed to spring to life as he entered the *dojo,* and his disciples marveled at how much bigger he appeared in his training uniform. Morihei was frequently smiling and laughing, but when he performed *misogi-no-jo* or held a sword, he was no longer a human being but a vehicle for the Great Spirit of Aiki. His eyes flashed, energy radiated from his body, and all became deathly still. "When he held a sword," his disciples relate, "he turned into one of those wrathful deities that slay evil."

Morihei was indifferent to organizational problems and handled the presentations of licenses and later *dan* rankings rather haphazardly. As noted above, he was only briefly under the auspices of the Daito Ryu and never possessed the full teaching license of that *ryu.* He gave *mokuroku* ("catalogue of techniques") to a few of the early disciples and/or copies of *Budo renshu* and *Budo* to others as a kind of license. When Kobukan instructors began teaching at outside institutions, they needed credentials and were subsequently supplied with *dan* rankings similar to those of *judo*. (A number of old-timers were unaware that the Headquarters Dojo had issued them such rankings.) Following the establishment of the Aikikai in 1948, a regular *kyu-dan* ranking system was instituted. Evidently, Morihei considered the eighth *dan* rank equivalent to the *menkyo-kaiden* teaching license of the old martial arts systems and awarded this rank to his top prewar and postwar disciples. Several others received ninth and even tenth *dan* ranks from Morihei, who tended to hand out such favors to those whom he liked and who asked for them. Among Morihei's senior disciples, the question of who received what rank and why is, and will likely remain, muddled.

Throughout his career, Morihei was constantly refining and expanding his art—"This old man must still train and train," he said not long before his death—and thus taught differently at different stages of his life. There is a definite continuum between prewar and postwar Aikido, but the techniques themselves evolved considerably. Morihei gave his disciples permission to film his techniques but warned, "Today's techniques will be different tomorrow." Hence, there is no standard Aikido; each of the direct disciples focused on those aspects he most readily understood and with which he had the most affinity, and then went on to develop an individual style based on his own experiences. Morihei encouraged this: "Learn one technique, and create ten or twenty more. Aikido is limitless." Given the great differences, though, it is sometimes hard to believe that all of them sat at the feet of the same master. The best advice in judging the different interpretations of Aikido is this: "Do not look for the differences; look for what is the same."

Individual training (*suburi*) and pair practice (*kumi-tachi*) are indispensable in Aikido. (*Left*) Morihei training in *tanren-uchi*, striking a heavy sword against a thick stack of branches, in Iwama. (*Below*) Morihei against a sword attack using his own weapon as an extension of his body, adjusting perfectly to his opponent's movements.

Prior to leading the training Morihei performed *misogi-no-jo* to restore his link to the divine and purify the *dojo*. *Misogi-no-jo* is a sacred dance, performed with the four-foot staff, that cleanses the area of evil and aligns body-mind-*ki*, form-spirit-divinity. The signboard above Morihei expresses a Zen sentiment: "Outside the mind there is no Dharma."

Morihei's techniques changed over the years. (*Left*) In his fifties, Morihei held the sword aggressively, up and out toward his opponent's head. (*Right*) In his final years, the sword sank to a deeper level, allowing Morihei to move from underneath to prevent his opponent from striking.

Morihei demonstrating the no-sword technique and the stance of no-stance. (*Top*) Morihei, with his body turned slightly to the right, is perfectly poised, and his softly focused gaze envelopes his armed opponent. His stance is solid but not at all static—it is 100 percent natural, and he seems to be inviting the swordsman to strike. Morihei displays here *fudo-shin,* "an immovable mind," which can respond to any contingency without a loss of composure. (*Bottom*) As soon as the attack commences, Morihei moves in with *irimi* directly toward his opponent's vital spots with just the right amount of movement—neither too fast nor too slow: "There is no time and space in Aikido—the techniques must arise right where you are."

3

A DETAILED DISCUSSION of the technical aspects of Aikido appears in my book *Aikido: The Way of Harmony* (Boston: Shambhala Publications, 1984) and in dozens of others. Here I will limit myself to a few salient points regarding techniques that are practiced universally in every Aikido *dojo*.

Despite the countless changes that Morihei's art underwent over the decades, four pivotal techniques remained at the core: *irimi, tenkan, shiho-nage,* and *suwari-ikkyo.*

Throughout his life, Morihei had a real affinity for thrusting weapons. In his youth, it was the harpoon; in his middle years, it was the bayonet and spear; in his last years, the *jo. Irimi,* "entering," and *issoku irimi,* "one-step entering," evolved from the study of those weapons. In *Budo* Morihei instructed, "When facing an opponent armed with a sword, stand squarely between life and death; remain calm and do not be confounded by the enemy or his weapon. Without a single opening, move decisively with *irimi* and obliterate the opponent's evil intentions." As soon as an attack arises, one immediately avoids the aggression by entering the "opening" inevitably created by that hostility. When executing the technique properly, one blends perfectly with an attack, countering it with a burst of concentrated energy, in the form of either a devastating *atemi,* as in the old days, or a gentler throw, as in modern times. Morihei left several important *doka* on the principle of *irimi:*

> *Seeing me before him*
> *the enemy attacks,*
> *but in a flash*
> *I am already*
> *standing behind him.*

> *Without the slightest opening*
> *no-mindedly ignore*
> *the attacking swords*

of your enemies—
step in and cut!

Left and right
avoid all
cuts and parries;
seize the opponent's mind
and enter directly!

Aikido is perhaps the only martial art that is truly open—attacks are always expected from all sides, and even when one is practicing with a single partner, attention is not focused exclusively on that individual.

Even when called out
by a single foe,
remain on guard,
for you are always surrounded
by a host of enemies.

The best method in dealing with a group attack is first *irimi,* to get out of the middle, and then *tenkan,* to neutralize the onslaught.

Tenkan, "turning," is the second pillar of Aikido. In *tenkan* the attack is neutralized by a circular movement, directing it around one's center, much like a spinning top rotating around a stable middle. One ends up facing the same direction as the attacker, leaving him no room to maneuver. The two complementary movements of *irimi* and *tenkan* are characterized as front and back (*omote* and *ura*), positive and negative (*yin* and *yang*), hard and soft, fire and water. It should also be noted that, ideally, one never blocks or otherwise receives an attack directly; it should always be turned back with *irimi* or turned around with *tenkan* so that the opponent can be led to a safe spot.

By keeping yang
in your right hand
and turning yin
with your left hand,
you can lead the enemy.

In the Aiki-Budo period, Morihei's *irimi-nage* was an explosive step out of the line of attack with an immediate countertechnique. In the later stages of his career, he tended to spin the opponent around with a *tenkan* turn and then bring him down softly with a

(*Top*) Morihei performing *tai-no-henko*, turning his opponent's aggression around and neutralizing the attack; one blends with the opponent so that both end up facing the same direction. (*Bottom*) Surrounded, Morihei executes the *irimi* movement to escape the circle of attackers and *tenkan* to turn it around him. In Aikido, practitioners always expect such eight-sided attacks.

circular *irimi* movement. (It was of course never performed exactly the same way twice.) This *en-no-irimi* is unique to Aikido and epitomizes the essence of the art—attuning one's mind and body to the natural rotating pulses that spin the universe. *En-no-irimi* is also the most difficult technique to master.

Although *shiho-nage*-like throws are found in other martial arts, Morihei explained Aikido's "four-directions throw" in terms of "four-directions cut" (*shiho-giri*), which in turn was based on the ancient imperial ceremony of "four-directions worship" (*shiho-hai*). On New Year's Day the emperor would pay his respects to the four directions of the universe, thanking the heavenly and earthly powers for past munificence and beseeching them for their continued favor. He was expressing his gratitude and respect. The "four" in *shiho-nage*, Morihei taught, "symbolizes the Four Gratitudes: gratitude toward the Divine, from which we received our animating spirit; gratitude toward our parents, from whom we received our body; gratitude toward nature, from which we receive our sustenance; and gratitude toward our fellow beings, from whom we receive life's daily necessities." In short, we cannot survive without the assistance of others and must never cease to be grateful in "four directions."

If *irimi-tenkan* is symbolized by a circle and *shiho-nage* by a square, then *suwari-ikkyo*, "pin number one," is symbolized by a triangle. One sits triangularly and must pin the opponent three-pointedly. Seated techniques were an absolute requirement in samurai times but long ago lost any practical applicability; nonetheless, Morihei insisted that such techniques continue to be practiced in Aikido, even in the early days at Iwama when there were no *tatami* and trainees had to practice on the bare floor. There is no other way to build strong legs and powerful, stable hips; also, human beings need to be reminded of the necessity of approaching the Divine on their knees with proper humility and graceful bearing. When Morihei was unable to lead the training personally, he preferred that his disciples practice seated rather than standing techniques—it is more difficult to become sloppy with one's footwork in seated techniques. Morihei placed so much importance on *suwari-ikkyo* that he sometimes had his disciples practice it for the entire hour of training. He also stressed the value of having one's joints stretched and stimulated by *ikkyo* and the other derivative pins: "They cleanse your stiff joints of accumulated dirt."

If *irimi, tenkan, shiho-nage,* and *suwari ikkyo* are the prime outer factors of Aikido, *kokyu-ho, ki-no-nagare, ki-musubi,* and *aiki* are the key inner factors. *Kokyu-ho,* the art of coordinating one's breath with that of Heaven, Earth, and one's partner, is fostered through a special set of techniques, typically practiced at the beginning and end of a training session. *Ki-no-nagare,* generally undertaken only after extensive training in basic solid techniques, is a heightened sensitivity to the flow of *ki* between oneself and one's partners. *Ki-no-nagare* techniques are characterized by free-flowing movements. *Ki-musubi* means "linking oneself to one's partner," tying up one's *ki* to another's in a

Morihei demonstrating *ikkyo,* source of all Aikido pinning techniques. The opponent is carried down with a triangular entry and a four-cornered pin. Morihei could bring his opponent down and hold him there with a single finger.

seamless unity. *Aiki,* "bringing together of *ki,*" is similar to *ki-musubi,* albeit with more emphasis on timing and harmonization of a conflicting force. *Aiki* is positioning oneself in exactly the right place. In sword partner practice, for instance, the more experienced partner receives the attack first because he or she is better able to adjust more naturally to whatever direction the attack takes; this is *aiki,* harmonization.

Another outstanding feature of Aikido is its distinctive breakfalls (*ukemi*). Advanced trainees fly through the air yet hit the mat with barely a sound and then spring up for more. One prominent present-day instructor, originally a *judo* man, decided to switch to Aikido after witnessing the spectacular falls: "The techniques may be fake," he thought, "but those breakfalls are unbelievable."

Once at the Kobukan, a master swordsman challenged Morihei; Morihei sidestepped the furious attack, and the swordsman's momentum carried him crashing into the *dojo* wall. His shoulder was so severely injured that he was obliged to abandon the practice of the martial arts altogether. Thereafter Morihei instructed his disciples to take breakfalls like a cat. "You should be able to take *ukemi* on any surface, even a stone floor." Morihei repeatedly stressed that the quickest way to make progress was to be an *uke* (receiver) for at least three years, actively experiencing the techniques in a direct and concrete manner. Those who refuse to be thrown will never advance. Morihei practiced what he preached. There is a delightful film clip of the seventy-five-year-old Morihei taking *ukemi* for one of his elementary school students.

Incidentally, several members of the imperial family joined a few of the classes held in Tokyo before the war. Morihei felt that it would be disrespectful to throw them on their royal rear ends, so he either immobilized them with a single finger or spun them around and not down.

In another prewar incident, one of Morihei's older friends, Dr. Futaki, who was then in his seventies, came to the *dojo* early every morning to rouse the live-in disciples by throwing them over and over. Morihei told the disciples to humor the old gentleman, for it was good breakfall training; the disciples, however, got a bit tired of being rolled repeatedly and planned to turn the tables suddenly and pin Dr. Futaki. Just as they were about to surprise the early-morning invader, Morihei popped into the *dojo* and announced, "That's enough for today."

Morihei gave the following instructions to his disciples:

> Aikido cannot be explained with words; one must practice and attain enlightenment of mind and body. Aikido training is not a sport nor asceticism; it is an act of faith based on the desire to achieve total awakening. Do not be in a hurry, for it takes a minimum of ten years to master the basics and advance to the first rung. Never think of yourselves as all-knowing, perfected instructors; you must continue to train daily with your students and progress together on the Path of Aiki.

Morihei's dictum that ten years are required to get a handle on the basics brings to mind a famous samurai tale:

A young man petitioned a great swordsman to admit him as a disciple. "I'll act as your servant and train ceaselessly. How long will it take me to learn everything?"

"At least ten years," the master replied.

"That's too long," the young man protested. "Suppose I work twice as hard as everyone else. Then how long will it take?"

"Thirty years," he was told.

"What do you mean?" he exclaimed. "I'll do anything to master swordsmanship as quickly as possible!"

"In that case, the master said sharply, "you will need fifty years. A person who is in such a hurry is a poor student."

The young man was eventually allowed to serve as an attendant on condition that he neither ask about nor touch a sword. After three years, the master began sneaking up on the young man at all hours of the day and night to whack him with his wooden sword. This continued until the young man could anticipate the attacks. Only then did formal instructions begin.

Similarly in Morihei's *dojo,* novices were set to work cleaning and doing other chores and taking breakfalls for the senior students. At the Kobukan it was often six months before a new trainee could actually try his hand at some of the techniques.

The two factors that distinguish Aikido from the other martial arts and from competitive sports are, respectively, that (1) the techniques are "alive," not bound by rules or rigid form, and (2) there are no contests. Classical martial arts insist that the traditional forms be preserved and transmitted intact. The techniques of Aikido, on the contrary, change each time they are performed, reflecting the physical and spiritual maturity of the practitioners. As one's level of understanding deepens, one's techniques undergo similar modification and improvement. Aikido is thus created anew each day, and the insights gained in the *dojo* must be applied to the multifarious problems of life.

Harmonization is the goal of Aikido, and the techniques are the vehicles that enable practitioners to test those principles, not in a show of strength and competition but in mutual accord and assistance. Each partner takes a turn assuming the role of attacker and defender; the techniques are always balanced between left and right, back and front, in and out.

Other martial artists are often critical of the Aikido bow: "One should never take one's eyes off an opponent." Aikido practitioners implicitly trust each other and display that mutual faith by bowing all the way to the floor and, as it were, offering their necks. When one bows before a shrine, one never suspiciously watches out for a surprise attack by the deity. In Aikido, one's partner is a "living shrine," due the same respect as a holy object. Indeed, "the practice of Aikido begins and ends with respect."

Once, in the prewar days, Morihei attended a joint martial arts demonstration held deep in the country. Afterward, he and several other *judo* and *kendo* instructors were returning to their inn along a farm road. The owner of those particular fields was a notoriously bad-tempered man. As soon as he noticed the intruders, he hurled a big lump of manure at them.

"Who do you think you are, trespassing on my property!" the farmer yelled.

"Who do you think you're talking to?" several members of the group shouted back as they moved toward the belligerent farmer.

The farmer then grabbed a bucket of manure to defend himself, but Morihei waved the others back and stepped forward alone.

"Why are you trespassing on my land?" the farmer demanded to know.

"We are sorry," Morihei apologized. "We were unaware that this is private property. Please forgive us." Morihei bowed deeply.

The nonplussed farmer was speechless as he watched Morihei lead the group away.

"Ueshiba Sensei," the others asked, "why did you let that hillbilly get away with such rudeness? You should have let us take care of him."

"It is foolish to create disturbances over trifles," Morihei replied thoughtfully. "Repaying violence with violence is always counterproductive; purifying oneself and others of violence and hate is the Way of Harmony."

Aikido is both harmony and love and must never degenerate into mere fighting and competition. Needless to say, given the instinct to survive at all costs and the innate desire to compete, supreme effort is required to suppress the urge to come out on top. Several of Morihei's senior disciples broke openly with their master on this point, insisting that organized competition was absolutely necessary for the development of Aikido as a modern sport. That type of thinking sorely distressed Morihei because, while there are hundreds of arenas in which to fight, athletics that provide guidance in harmonization and love are precious few. Morihei said:

> From ancient times, *budo* has never been considered a sport. If there are contests, we must be ready to kill. Those who seek competition are making a grave mistake. To smash, injure, or destroy is the worst sin a human being can commit. The old saying "The martial deities never kill" is true. Real *budo* is a Path of Peace.

PART THREE

The Message

Aikido is the manifestation of Love.
—MORIHEI UESHIBA

I

MORIHEI'S SEARCH for the true meaning of *budo* was far more than a physical challenge; it was an intense spiritual journey as well.

Japanese spirituality is divided into two broad streams. There is the Zen stream: bold, direct, austere. Physical and intellectual baggage is kept at an absolute minimum; insight is fostered through deep introspection, self-control, and nonattachment to objects, ideas, and events—in a word, Buddhist emptiness. The other side of the circle is the mystical stream: divinity can be attained through the practice of secret rites, trance, and transmutation. Here, there is an acute awareness of the sacred and the profane; revelation, prophecy, and shamanism take center stage.

Morihei's mind-set was rooted in the second stream. From his early belief in the cult gods of Kumano, his initiation into the profundities of Shingon, and his infatuation with Omoto-kyo occultism, Morihei was in continual communication with the gods, fairies, and gremlins of old Japan.

Contrary to popular belief, Morihei neither studied Zen nor employed its methods or terminology in his teaching. It is often argued that while the respective approaches differ, the goal of Zen and mysticism is the same: liberation of the human spirit. True, the famous Buddhist scholar D. T. Suzuki called Aikido "moving Zen," many Zen devotees enjoy practicing Aikido as a complement to their seated meditation, and there are several high-ranking instructors who are Buddhist priests; but the framework of the art of Aikido as conceived by Morihei reflects a world view that has almost nothing in common with Zen in particular or Buddhism in general.

Morihei was caught up in the tumultuous revival of the ancient forms of Japanese religion during the nineteenth and twentieth centuries. Following the Meiji Restoration in 1868, there was a renewed interest in both esoteric (epitomized by Omoto-kyo) and exoteric (state) Shinto. Buddhism was widely attacked as a foreign creed, and efforts were made to purge Japanese thought of such an alien system. (Such an attitude has not entirely disappeared. In a recent book on traditional Shinto this statement appears: "Buddhism, particularly Zen, is the antithesis of Japanese religion and art.") Although

Morihei lecturing on the spiritual world of Aikido. All agree that they could not make any sense of Morihei's baffling sermons at the time; some, however, have said that the meaning gradually became clearer the longer they trained.

Omoto-kyo retained certain Buddhist elements, its tenets are about as far removed from Zen as one can get.

(The Japanese martial arts are similarly divided into a Zen and a mystical stream. Zen is closely identified with Musashi, Yagyu, and above all Tesshu. Other schools, including Katori Shinto Ryu and Aikido, are Shinto-oriented in outlook.)

What follows is an attempt to present Aikido as it was actually perceived by Morihei himself. This is not easy. Morihei's own explanations were maddeningly abstruse. He rambled from one subject to another, rattling off the names of obscure Shinto deities, stringing together combinations of baffling terms, and offering idiosyncratic interpretations of Japanese history, interspersed with totally irrelevant reminiscences of past events. His talks were such a confused jumble that it has been suggested that Morihei was, on those occasions, "speaking in tongues," possessed by one *kami* or another. Most of his ideas are derived from impossibly complex Omoto-kyo doctrine and Morihei's reading of Japan's oldest chronicle, the *Kojiki* ("Record of Ancient Matters").

Morihei's interest in the *Kojiki* was based on his devotion to *kotodama* theory (discussed in the next section). Proper recitation of the verses, apparent gibberish to the uninitiated, enables one to grasp the text's magical properties. Morihei, imbued from birth in Shinto lore, was inspired by the *Kojiki*, but it is extremely difficult for those with different backgrounds (including modern Japanese) to generate much enthusiasm for this collection of strange myths and bizarre tales.

Rather than focus on every word of Morihei's and getting bogged down in arcane minutiae, it is necessary to cut through the mass of culturally conditioned excess and present Morihei's message in universally comprehensible terms.

2

FIRST OF ALL, Morihei regarded Aikido not as his own creation but as a holy path that was revealed to him as a mirror of the divine ordinance of the universe. Morihei stressed the revolutionary impact of Aikido, the martial art of peace and harmony for the New Age, an era in which spiritual and not physical force will ultimately triumph.

> *The three thousand worlds*
> *are revealed at once;*
> *a plum blossom blooms*
> *and the stone door will be*
> *opened a second time.*

Aikido, a rare flower that is in full bloom for the first time, illuminates the workings of the universe. The stone door, a reference to a Shinto myth in which the goddess of light was enticed from the underground to shine again on the earth, will be opened by the combined efforts of good people everywhere, and the polluted world of death and destruction will be bathed once more in the sunbeams of truth and beauty. The purpose of Aikido, Morihei maintained, "is to build a heaven on earth by bringing people together in friendship and harmony. I teach this art to help my students learn how to serve their fellow beings."

Further, Morihei stated, "Aikido is the religion that is not a religion; rather it perfects and completes all religions. From the time that you rise in the morning to the time you retire for the night, you must follow the Path of Aiki and pursue the harmonization of the world and all its inhabitants."

> *Protector of this world*
> *and guardian of the ways*
> *of gods and buddhas,*
> *the techniques of Aiki*
> *enable us to meet every challenge.*

Morihei generally elaborated his system in terms of *kotodama,* the science of "sound-spirit." Kotodama theory was at the heart of the Shinto revival, based on the supposedly pure sounds of the unique Japanese language. In fact, the concept of *kotodama* originates in the tantric *sphota-vada* system of ancient India which was carried to Japan by the Buddhist patriarch Kukai in the ninth century as *shingon,* "true sounds."

The Supreme Word (Skt. *sabda brahman,* Jap. *su*) is the innermost core of being. In Christian theology this is expressed as "In the beginning was the Word and the Word was with God." From that Word Supreme, fifty pure sounds (Skt., *varna,* Jap. *koto*) sprang forth (Skt. *sphota,* Jap. *musubu*), crystallizing as vibrations (Skt. *nada,* Jap. *hibiki*) of various concentrations that are perceived as sound, color, and form—that is, the phenomenal world. Those sound-spirits, imbued with cosmic energy (Skt. *shakti, prana,* Jap. *ki, kokyu*), activate and sustain creation.

The tantric concept of the universe being composed of sound-energy formed the basis of Hindu and Buddhist *mantrayana* and Japanese Shinto *kotodama* theory; *kotodama* was in turn further modified by Onisaburo in his Omoto-kyo teachings and then adopted by Morihei for Aikido.

In Aikido *kotodama* theory, the universe is said to have originated from an incomprehensibly dense point, represented by the ultraconcentrated vibration *su.* Aeons ago, steam, smoke, and mist emanated from that point, enveloping it in a nebulous sphere. From *su,* the primordial *kotodama* point, the sound of cosmic inhalation, energy-sound-breath, simultaneously spiraled forth. *Su* extended circularly into the sounds u-u-u-yu-mu and also expanded vertically into the sounds a-o-u-e-i. The tension between these sounds gave birth to spirit-matter, fire-water, *yin-yang,* and further evolved into the seventy-five *kotodama* that maintain existence.

This cosmology—strikingly similar to the Big Bang theory currently favored by physicists—was further detailed by Morihei as "one source, four spirits, three elements, and eight powers" (*ichirei-shikon-sangen-hachiriki*). "One source" is the single point *su* referred to above, and the other elements can be diagramed as follows:

FOUR SPIRITS
1. *Kusu-mitama:* heaven, wisdom, light, principle
2. *Ara-mitama:* fire, valor, progress, completion
3. *Nigi-mitama:* water, fidelity, harmony, propriety
4. *Sachi-mitama:* earth, love, compassion, cherishing

THREE SOURCES
1. *Iku-musubi:* harmonization, vapor, fluidity; represented by a triangle

2. *Taru-musubi:* inhalation, liquid, unification; represented by a circle
3. *Tamatsume-musubi:* exhalation, solid, solidity; represented by a square

EIGHT POWERS
1. Movement
2. Calm
3. Solidification
4. Release
5. Extension
6. Retraction
7. Unification
8. Division

Schematically the entire system can be rendered as in the accompanying diagram. Through the interaction of these sounds the universe sprang into being. Every principle, according to *kotodama,* has a sacred seed sound, which contains its essence; if

THE HEAVENLY TECHNIQUE OF TAKEMUSU AIKI

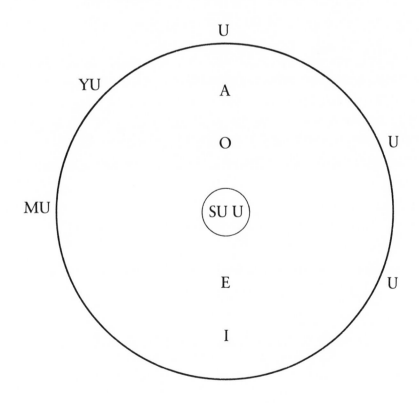

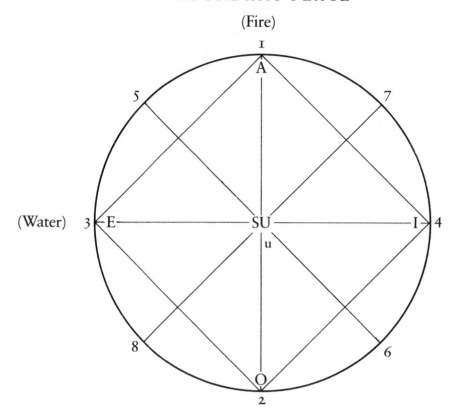

one knows the significance of the sound, one can understand its function and thereby merge with its spirit. A tantric text puts it this way:

> Taking a stand on the essence of the Word lying beyond the activity of breath, one rests in oneself with all sequence eliminated. After purifying speech and retaining it in mind, after breaking all bonds and being liberated, after reaching the inner light, one with his bonds cut becomes united with the Supreme.

By way of illustration, consider the concept of *taka-ama-hara*, to which Morihei frequently referred in his talks. Mythologically, *taka-ama-hara* means "the High Plain of Heaven" (where the Shinto gods dwell). In terms of *kotodama*, however, the phrase re-creates the formation and functioning of the universe: *ta* = harmonization → *ka* = sustenance → *a* = manifestation → *ma* = life → *ha* = activity → *ra* = fecundity. *Taka-ama-hara* is thus a pure state of mind without anomaly or excess.

Further extending *kotodama* wordplay, the character *hara* ("plain") is replaced with the character *hara* ("abdomen"), indicating that heaven is not up in the sky but in the pit of one's being, the "red blood boiling within one's *hara*" as Morihei called the *kotodama* that summoned up his divine strength. Prior to training, Morihei would emit an eerie *kotodama* sound to activate the flow of energy and light. His eyes would flash and he seemed to expand mightily into a different dimension, taken hold of, as it were, by the *kotodama* he had called forth.

> *Source of all,*
> *origin of the*
> *seventy-five [kotodama],*
> *merciful teacher of*
> *the Path of Aiki.*

Morihei never tired of reiterating: "One's body is a miniature universe." The notion that all that exists in the universe must also exist in one's body is common to Tantra— "What is here is there; what is not here is nowhere"—and to Buddhism—"In this very body, Buddha declared, six feet in length, with its sense impressions, its thoughts, and its ideas are the world, the origin of the world, and the ceasing of the world."

Parallel to the insight that "I am the Universe" is the realization that "I am nothing"; that is to say, not a separate entity existing independently from the vastness of creation. Morihei exclaimed: "The essence of Aikido is zero."

Morihei pronouncing a *kotodama* sound from the center of his being. Notice how he places his hand over the core of his body, where the "boiling red blood" is being called forth, expanding mightily as the *kotodama* spirals upward.

If you do not blend
with the emptiness of
the Pure Void,
you will never know
the Path of Aiki.

He also said:

> Unite yourself to the cosmos, and the thought of transcendence will disappear. Transcendence belongs to the profane world; when all trace of transcendence vanishes, the true person—the Divine Being—is manifest. Empty yourself and let the Divine function.

The *kami* of which Morihei spoke so frequently can be understood in the following manner: the cosmos is activated and sustained through the interaction of *ka* (fire) and *mi* (water). Functioning in accordance with *aiki*, fire and water (*kami*) particularize into the myriad forms of the phenomenal world. The purest concentrations of fire and water are *kami*, powers that provide the sustenance for life. Such *kami* range in dimension from the *o-kami,* the great gods of time, space, and being, to innumerable lesser *kami,* including human beings that animate little corners of the world.

As a Shinto shaman, Morihei was convinced that he was vouchsafed a visit from his guardian deities Ame-no-murakumo-kuki-samuhara-ryu-o (the first word is sometimes pronounced *Ama*) and Ta-jikara-ono-mikoto one evening when he was in his early forties and that they subsequently possessed him. Not surprisingly, Morihei was electrified by this mind-shattering vision, but after he recovered from the shock he found that he was superhumanly strong. According to *kotodama* science, *Ame-no-murakumo-kuki-samuhara-ryu-o* translates as follows: universal *ki* (*ame-no-murakumo*) is procreated (*kuki*) and structured (*samuhara*) by the protector and sustainer of life (the dragon king Ryu-o). In simpler terms, all this means that Morihei had a mystical experience in which he imagined himself to be a vessel of the divine energy of the cosmos. Thereafter, Morihei felt himself to be an incarnation of Ta-jikara-ono-mikoto, "Male Principle of Physical Strength."

In both mystical Shinto and esoteric Buddhism, it is firmly believed that masters, after years and years of the severest training, can actually perceive, with their inner eye of wisdom, the holy beings of the spiritual realms. The gods and buddhas of the pantheon reveal themselves interiorly to pure-minded practitioners such as Morihei:

> You cannot see or touch the Divine with your gross senses.
> The Divine is within you, not somewhere else. Unite your-

self to the Divine, and you will be able to perceive *kami*
wherever you are, but do not try to grasp or cling to them.

Shinto teaches that everyone is inherently a *kami;* the word *hito,* "human being,"
means the place where the spark of life rests. However, most people are either unaware
or forgetful of their divine birthright or too mired in pollution. *Chinkon-kishin,* an ancient Shinto meditation technique similar to the tantric visualizations of the Hindus and
Tibetans, was employed by Onisaburo and then Morihei as a means to "calm the spirit
and return to the Divine." *Chinkon,* "calming of the spirit," involves quietly centering
the body and mind through a series of *mudras* and invocations, preferably performed in
a holy spot. *Kishin,* "returning to the Godhead," is a trancelike state of mystical union
with the Divine. After becoming an Omoto-kyo follower, Morihei reverently performed
chinkon-kishin every morning and an abbreviated version prior to training.

Closely related to *chinkon-kishin* is the practice of *misogi,* ritual purification. The
custom of washing away impurities with cold water, if possible in a fast-flowing river
or beneath a waterfall, dates back to the dawn of Japanese religious consciousness, and
the practice plays an important role in Japanese creation myths and Shinto rites. Con-
tact with the dirt and dust of this imperfect world stains one's original pristine nature;
misogi purifies one of all the accumulated defilements and restores one's link to sacred
being. There is external *misogi,* in which one rinses off the body with cold water, and
internal *misogi,* in which one cleanses the inner organs with deep, regenerating breaths.
After performing *misogi* properly and aligning oneself once more with the wellsprings
of life, one can enter a state of *sumikiri,* "crystal clarity of body and mind." In that enlightened condition one's heart is as bright and clear as a cloudless sky, untainted by
base passions and worldly concerns.

> *Crystal clear,*
> *sharp and bright,*
> *my mind has*
> *no opening for*
> *evil to roost.*
>
> *The morning sun shines in,*
> *my mind, too, is clear and bright;*
> *from my window, I let myself*
> *soar to the highest heaven,*
> *bathed in divine light.*

Morihei did not like his non-Omoto-kyo disciples to ape his religious practices and
made those who were merely imitating his performance of *chinkon-kishin* and *misogi*

stop. Instead, Morihei specifically instructed his followers to utilize the pure techniques of Aikido as their form of worship. "Aikido is *misogi,* purification of body and mind, a Way to reform and transform the world. I show my techniques to encourage those of little faith." Morihei gave this advice:

> Daily training in Aikido allows your inner divinity to shine brighter and brighter. Do not concern yourself with the right and wrong of others. Keep the mind bright and clear as the endless sky, the deepest ocean, and the highest mountain. Do not be calculating or act unnaturally. Keep your mind set on Aikido, and do not criticize other teachers or traditions. Aikido never restrains, restricts, or shackles anything. It embraces all and purifies everything.
>
> > *Rely on Aiki*
> > *to activate your*
> > *manifold powers;*
> > *pacify all things and*
> > *create a beautiful world.*

3

THE KEY TO AIKIDO TECHNIQUES IS *KI*: "To train in Aiki one must drill in the development of *ki*. *Ki* is exceedingly complex, and we must risk our lives to master it." Although *ki* is a vital element of East Asian culure—in Oriental medicine, for instance, one is considered in good health when one's *ki* is strong and unimpeded but ill when one's *ki* is sluggish and dull—it is difficult to pin down conceptually. *Ki* is the subtle energy that propels the universe, the life force that holds things together. *Ki* appears to be quite similar to the "superstrings" that modern physicists believe tie together the basic forces of nature. Just as the superstrings are thought to constantly interact, coalescing into one, dividing into two, positive *ki* and negative *ki* continually unite and disperse within the great rotating wheel of existence.

Ki is inextricably bound with *kokyu,* cosmic breath. *Ki* radiates from *kokyu,* and *kokyu* is the vivifying force that activates *ki*. Everything in this world breathes, in one form or another; indeed, in Japanese to live (*iki*) is to breathe (*iki*). Exhalation is circular, a function of water; inhalation is square, a function of fire. Together they form *kokyu,* the characters of which, according to *kotodama,* can be read as *iki,* "animation." In Aikido, the ideal is to link one's breath to the cosmic flow of *kokyu;* breathing in unison with the cosmos, one is permeated with breath power (*kokyu-ryoku*).

Aiki is the harmonization (*ai*) of primal energies (*ki*); opposites—fire-water, *yin-yang,* heaven-earth, male-female, inhalation-exhalation, self-other—are brought together in creative unity. The phenomenal world is maintained through the subtle workings of *aiki;* when that delicate balance is overturned, there is chaos, destruction, and death.

While Morihei adopted his Aikido cosmology from Omoto-kyo, he learned the mechanics of *ki* harmonization and breath power from Sokaku. The Daito Ryu *kokyu-ho* techniques were carefully guarded secrets; once one was able to coordinate the outflow of *ki* with one's breath, he or she became a superior warrior. (It should be noted that *ki* and *kokyu* power are neutral forces that can be harnessed by anyone, independent of individual moral and spiritual qualities. *Aiki-jutsu* and *kiai-jutsu,* the art of downing an opponent with *ki* and *kokyu* power, should be clearly distinguished from Aikido, the path of spiritual integration and love.)

Morihei explaining the mysteries of *ki:* "Spread your fingertips and let your *ki* flow to the ends of the universe."

Prior to training, Morihei sat quietly before the Shinto altar to bring his *ki* and *kokyu* in tune with pulsating energy patterns of the universe, either by protracted pronunciation of a *kotodama* or by inhaling and exhaling the seed syllables *a* and *un*, which symbolize the alpha and omega of existence. In short, Morihei and, by extension, all Aikido practitioners seek harmonization of body-mind-*ki-kokyu;* if one is bound to the dynamic rhythm of the universe, he or she can move without resistance anywhere, anytime—the essence of Aikido.

> *Bind yourself up*
> *with* ki,
> *stand in the center,*
> *polish your mind,*
> *and be engulfed by divine vibrations.*
>
> *The wonderful workings of* ki
> *create techniques to purify*
> *body and mind.*
> *Guide us,*
> *O gods of heaven and earth!*
>
> *Master the divine*
> *techniques of* ki,
> *and no enemy*
> *will dare to*
> *challenge you.*

Morihei's mature philosophy was expressed in the phrase *Takemusu Aiki.*

> I discovered by reading Shinto texts that *Takemusu* is the heart of Japanese *budo*—totally free and capable of unlimited transformations. Universal and particular function harmoniously in Takemusu Aiki.

Take, also pronounced *bu,* is "martial valor"; Morihei taught that it is the wisdom, bravery, compassion, and love that protect and nourish all things. *Musu* is derived from *musubu,* the procreative force of existence—fecund, life-generating, irrepressibly productive. Taken together, *Takemusu Aiki* stands for the unlimited creativity of Aikido.

> Aiki is not an art to fight with or to defeat an enemy. It is a Way in which to harmonize all people into one family. The

essence of Aikido is put to oneself in tune with the functioning of the universe, to become one with the universe. Those who have grasped the inner meaning of Aikido possess the universe within themselves.

Regardless of how quickly an opponent attacks or how slowly I respond, I cannot be defeated. It is not that my techniques are faster than those of my opponent. It has nothing to do with speed or slowness. I am victorious right from the start. As soon as the thought of attack crosses my opponent's mind, he shatters the harmony of the universe and is instantly defeated regardless of how quickly he attacks. Victory or defeat is not a matter of time or space.

Aikido is the principle of nonresistance. Because it is nonresistant, it is victorious from the beginning. Those with evil intentions or contentious thoughts are instantly vanquished. True *budo* is invincible since it contends with nothing.

In his final years, Morihei equated *ai*, "harmony," with *ai*, "love."

Above all, one must unite one's heart with that of the gods. The essence of God is love, an all-pervading love that reaches every corner of the universe. If one is not united to God, the universe cannot be harmonized. Martial artists who are not in harmony with the universe are merely executing combat techniques, not Takemusu Aiki.

The Way is like the flow of blood in one's veins. A hair's-breadth of separation between yourself and the Mind of God and you are no longer on the Path of Aiki.

In true *budo,* there are no enemies. True *budo* is a function of love. It is not for killing or fighting but to foster all things and bring them to fruition. Love protects and nourishes life. Without love nothing can be accomplished. Aikido is the manifestation of love.

THE MESSAGE

The lovely form of
Heaven and Earth
lovingly created
by the Great God,
Father of Humankind.

When Morihei spoke of God, he was referring to Ame-no-minaka-nushi, the Creator of the Universe, the Word Supreme at the center of the great cosmic pouring-forth. Unlike the cruder forms of fundamentalist theology, East and West, in which God is conceived as being somewhere "out there," ensconced in Paradise or a Pure Land, Morihei's system views God as being "in here," a sacred flame within one's body. Aikido is a type of pantheism since it breaks down the artificial barriers between gods and humans, the individual soul and the world-soul, emptiness and form.

Morihei often spoke of "standing on the floating bridge of heaven" between the physical and spiritual worlds. In Aikido, the distinction between the three worlds—manifest, hidden, divine—is overturned and all three realms are made accessible. (The manifest is the world of form in front of our eyes; the hidden is the invisible fields of energy and atoms; the divine is the source of inspiration and enlightenment.)

Newcomers to Aikido can see nothing but the manifested techniques (many in fact never progress beyond this level); experienced practitioners eventually grasp the hidden factors of *ki, kokyu,* and *aiki*. Morihei discerned the divine characteristics of the movements, thus blending the manifest, hidden, and divine into an art that is beautiful, true, beneficial, and pleasant.

Near the end of his life, Morihei brushed this calligraphic summing-up of Aikido:

> Manifest, hidden, divine: three worlds [revealed] through
> the joyous Path of Love.

If we train sincerely, day in and day out, in the spirit of Aiki, perhaps we too can partake in that grand vision, sport in the paradise of the three worlds, and experience the ineffable bliss of the joyous Path of Love.

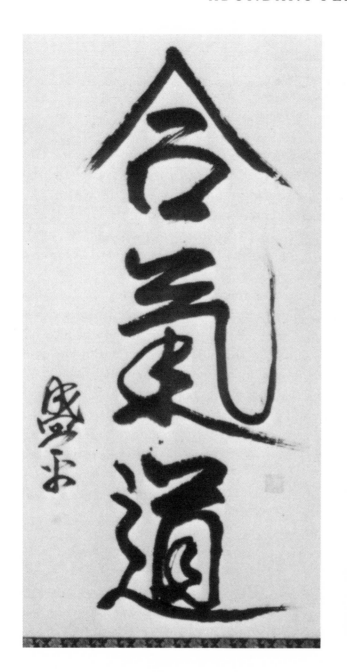

Like most Oriental masters, Morihei left behind an important legacy in the form of calligraphy. "Calligraphy is the person" is a famous saying, and the belief that one lives in his or her brushwork is prevalent in East Asia. Morihei brushed numerous pieces to inspire and instruct his disciples. He did calligraphs of *Aikido*, naturally—one of these (*far left*) is permanently displayed in the main *dojo* of the headquarters—but generally presented *Aiki Okami* (*left*) and *Takemusu Aiki* (*top*) to his top disciples. Aiki Okami and Takemusu are the source of Aikido, and we can imagine that Morihei was telling his disciples to look beyond the form and capture the spirit. When he visited a branch *dojo*, Morihei often brushed smaller calligraphy boards on the spur of the moment. (*Bottom*) This board reads: "The brillance of *bu*." Interestingly, Morihei frequently sealed his works with *Aiki Jinja*, as if he had completely identified with that shrine. The works at left and top date from Morihei's seventies, when he was using the name Tsunemori; the other two examples, from his eighties, are signed *Morihei*.

4

HAVING PRESENTED MORIHEI'S PHILOSOPHY in his own terms, I would like to discuss Aikido within the context of the traditional martial arts.

The base instinct of aggression drives people to fight and go to war. The innate reaction to protect oneself results in the arts of self-defense. The dream of living in peace and harmony compels warriors to seek a path out of the turmoil of death and destruction.

East and West, reflective human beings have always been aware that fighting and killing are evil. "Those that live by the sword will perish by the sword," Jesus declared two millennia ago; the ancient Chinese character for "martial," when broken down into its components, means "to stop two halberds"—that is, to quell violence and maintain peace.

Even in war-torn medieval Japan, when the foremost thought of most warriors was to slay an opponent with a decisive cut of a razor-sharp blade, there were thoughtful samurai who perceived that killing was not the essence of the Way of the Sword. For example, we have this story about Bokuden Tsukahara, one of the swordsmen mentioned by Morihei in *Budo renshu:*

Once Bokuden happened to be on a small ferry boat when another swordsman began boasting of his prowess. While the braggart carried on, Bokuden dozed off. This angered the other swordsman so that he shook Bokuden, demanding to know what style he followed. When Bokuden replied, "The Victory-without-using-one's-hands School," the rowdy swordsman challenged Bokuden to display such techniques. Bokuden agreed but suggested that they stop at an island to conduct the match so as to avoid injury to the other passengers. The ferryboat made a detour to a nearby island. As soon as the boat reached the shore, the ruffian leaped off, drew his sword, and assumed his stance. Bokuden stood up and appeared to follow his opponent when he suddenly grabbed an oar and precipitately pushed the boat back into the river. He yelled to the stranded swordsman, "This is defeating an enemy without using your hands!

While Morihei identified with Bokuden, he had, like many martial artists, a rather low opinion of the fabled Miyamoto Musashi. Despite his tremendous popularity as a folk hero, Musashi's ruthless cunning, wild behavior, and disregard for the sensibilities of polite samurai society earned him an unsavory reputation among conservative martial artists. In his youth, Musashi was obsessed with winning at any cost; he was an unrivaled strategist and marvelous technician, to be sure, but as he himself realized, there is much more to the Way of the Sword than slaughtering one's opponent.

Musashi retired from the battlefield and devoted himself to finding that which transcends winning and losing. Near the end of his life, Musashi was invited to serve the lord of the Kumamoto Domain. Not long after his arrival, Musashi was challenged to a contest by a Yagyu master. Musashi steadfastly refused, in spite of repeated requests, saying, "The day when I competed in matches is long past. I no longer have any desire to fight with others."

Nevertheless, Musashi's patron, the Lord of Kumamoto, finally prevailed upon him to accept. Musashi gave in, provided that only the Yagyu swordsman and the lord be present at the match and that all participants agree not to say anything about the outcome to others.

As soon as they came together, Musashi forced his opponent back with a penetrating shout and irresistible forward movement, completely preventing a response. The Yagyu swordsman tried twice again to face Musashi to a standstill, but to no avail. The lord had a go, but he too was totally stymied. Instead of smashing their skulls as he would have done without hesitation in the old days, Musashi kept them at bay with his superior *ki* power, and both he and his opponents escaped unharmed. (Despite the vow of secrecy, details of the contest leaked out.)

Still the smell of blood lingers: Musashi and a Zen priest were doing *zazen* late one night in Reigando, the cave in which Musashi sequestered himself during his final years. A huge poisonous snake entered the cave, slithered across the Zen priest's lap, and headed toward Musashi. Suddenly the snake reared up in alarm, paused for a second, and then raced out of the cave in a panic. Even though Musashi made no threatening gestures, the snake sensed a killer nearby.

Musashi represents the "killing sword" of steely resolve and calm acceptance of death, the so-called "body of a rock." Musashi was proud of his twenty-three-year-old adopted son's decision to commit *seppuku* in order to join his deceased lord in death, and praised a retainer in the Kumamoto lord's service who calmly accepted his master's (false) command to slit open his stomach.

Musashi may have exemplified the dictum that the duty of a samurai is "to learn how to die," but others rejected that notion and centered their ideals on the life-giving properties of *budo*.

The Yagyu Ryu promoted the life-giving sword in its teachings, and Morihei adopted both ideas and techniques from that School. In the *Heiho kaden sho*, Yagyu Munenori wrote: "Following years of training and discipline, one must forget all that one has learned. Lose yourself and the techniques will come forth freely. With a mind stuck nowhere, there is no place for evil to lurk. To become what one has learned, to go beyond memorization and cognition, is the secret of mastering any art."

Similarly, Morihei declared: "When I perform Aikido, I forget myself—all ego disappears."

The sword-taking techniques (*tachi-dori*) of Aikido are derived from Yagyu "no-sword" methods, that is, facing a swordsman unarmed. The Tokugawa Shogun Ieyasu once asked Yagyu Muneyoshi to demonstrate the no-sword techniques. Muneyoshi, unarmed, instructed the Shogun to attack with his sword. Ieyasu lashed out with a strike at Muneyoshi's head, but in an instant, Muneyoshi avoided the cut, grabbed the hilt of the sword, took the weapon away from the Shogun, and then gave Ieyasu a slight tap on the chest which sent him reeling backward. "Impressive indeed," exclaimed the stunned Shogun.

The Yagyu school held that weapons are to be used in only the most extreme situations and even then as instruments of divine retribution; an attacker of an enlightened warrior fell on the blade himself, carried there by his delusion and lack of self-control.

Regarding this, here is a tale told about Yagyu Mitsuyoshi (Jubei), the other swordsman mentioned by Morihei in *Budo renshu:* Once, at a local lord's manor, Mitsuyoshi was challenged to a match by another swordsman. They fought twice with bamboo swords, both matches seemingly ending in *ai-uchi,* simultaneously delivered blows.

Mitsuyoshi asked his opponent, "Are you aware of the outcome of these two contests?"

"They were draws," the swordsman replied proudly.

Mitsuyoshi asked the lord for his opinion.

"It appeared to me that they were draws."

A bit exasperated, Mitsuyoshi complained, "Doesn't anyone here see what really happened?"

Mitsuyoshi's opponent, certain that he had held the Yagyu master to a draw, shot back, "If you are so sure that it wasn't a draw, let's have another go at it—this time with live blades."

"Don't throw your life away," Mitsuyoshi retorted. "It is not worth it."

The enraged swordsman, his pride wounded, insisted.

"All right," Mitsuyoshi sighed. "Have it your way."

They leaped at each other, and the two flashing blades seemed to find their marks at the same time. Mitsuyoshi, however, remained erect with a slight cut on the outer layer of his kimono; his opponent fell dead to the ground with a huge gash halfway through his body.

"What a waste," Mitsuyoshi remarked sadly.

The nineteenth-century heir of the life-giving sword was Tesshu Yamaoka, founder of the Muto Ryu, the School of No-Sword. This amazing man—martial artist supreme, master calligrapher, and Zen master—is perhaps Morihei's only rival as Japan's greatest *budoka*. Well aware of the maxim "If your mind is correct, then your technique will be correct," Tesshu, like Morihei, emphasized the spiritual rather than the technical dimensions of swordsmanship. New entrants to Tesshu's Shumpukan Dojo were told: "The purpose of Muto Ryu swordsmanship is not to engage in contests nor to defeat others; training in my *dojo* is to foster enlightenment, and for this you must be willing to risk your life. Attack me any way you wish. Do not hold back!" After knocking the novice to the floor, generally with a tremendous thrust, Tesshu would shout, "Get up and come at me again!" This would continue until the candidate dropped from exhaustion. Tesshu might keep up such treatment for a week in order to test the determination of a prospective trainee. Technical ability did not matter at all—one of the top Shumpukan swordsmen was so uncoordinated that he was unable to swing a sword perfectly straight—and if the candidate's spirit was strong, he was selected for admittance. Tesshu proclaimed: "If single-minded determination is absent, one will never advance . . . technique has its place but spiritual forging is far more important."

Here are a few of Tesshu's *doka:*

*If your mind
is not projected
into your hands,
even ten thousand techniques
will be useless.*

*Against an opponent's sword
assume no stance,
and keep your mind unmoved;
that is the place
of victory.*

*Swordsmanship:
I am not struck,
nor is my opponent hit;
unobstructed, I move in
and attain the ultimate.*

*Where swords cross
throw off illusion;
abandon yourself
and you will tread
the living Path.*

This formal portrait of Morihei resembles a *chinzo,* a painting of a Buddhist patriarch that attempts to portray the spirit rather than the form of the teacher. Typically, the subject adds an inscription that sums up his career. Morihei's inscription on this portrait reveals exactly how he saw himself: *Haya-Takemusu-Okami, Ame-no-murakumo-kuki-samuhara-Ryu-o, Katsu-haya-bi-koka, Aiki-Tsunemori.* It would require another book to explain the esoteric significance of each word and phrase, but these mystic pronouncements can be simplified thus: Morihei is the messenger of the Great God Takemusu, who acts swiftly to right injustice; Morihei was designated by that god to descend to earth as a dynamic presence, putting things aright according to the eternal abundance of Aiki, and he is protected by the supreme Dragon King, a metaphor for the forces of nature brought under one's control. Morihei had a mission to unite the material, spiritual, and divine worlds through the virtue of Takemusu Aiki; he was ever-victorious because of his reliance on *Masakatsu-agatsu,* "True victory is self-victory."

Although Tesshu and Morihei never met—Tesshu died when Morihei was five years old—Morihei did have contacts with several of Tesshu's Muto Ryu disciples and likely absorbed some of that master's teachings. (There is a slight possibility that Sokaku met Tesshu. Several people, including the late Chief Justice Kazuto Ishida, studied both Daito Ryu and Muto Ryu, and Aikido instructor Koichi Tohei trained for a time under Tetsuju Ogura, a direct disciple of Tesshu. Also, Tesshu was one of the heroes of the Black Dragon Society, with which Morihei had a loose association during the prewar days;

such adulation by that ultranationalist organization is a bit puzzling since Tesshu was famed for dumping Meiji on his rear end when the inebriated emperor tried to engage Tesshu in a wrestling match, and he did not hesitate to lecture the sovereign in public.)

In spite of their many similarities, there were important differences between these two modern masters. First of all, Tesshu was an ardent Buddhist, largely responsible for the survival of Japanese Buddhism during the persecutions and Shinto revival of the early years of Meiji.

Tesshu's lively Zen Buddhism is much more accessible than Morihei's mind-boggling esotericism, which is nearly impossible for even the most avid student of Aikido to swallow hook, line, and sinker, if he or she can understand it at all. (Morihei never insisted that his followers accept his personal beliefs; quite the opposite—"Do not mimic me.") Also, Tesshu's openness to life in all of its manifestations, his unstinting charity, and his dynamic teaching methods make him perhaps a somewhat more appealing figure than the moody, hypersensitive, and fastidious Morihei.

On the other hand, Tesshu was unable to pass on his unbearably severe "sword of no-sword," and the Muto Ryu effectively ended with his death. In contrast, the applicability of Morihei's Aikido is universal, and the art has become widely acclaimed the world over.

In my view it is Tesshu who teaches the *budoka* how to "live completely" and Morihei who shows us the actual methods of embracing opposition with love.

5

I T IS PERHAPS NOT INCORRECT to think of Morihei as an avatar of the Great God of Aiki, appearing among us to reveal the Way of Harmony. Like any other person, Morihei had a human as well as divine side to his character. The earthly, imperfect elements withered away at his death, but the divine aspects remain with us in the form of Aikido.

Morihei opened a path for us, one that can be followed both physically and spiritually, but each person must tread it by himself or herself and each choose his or her own direction: "Aikido is a compass."

Although the Way of Harmony is all-inclusive, it is extremely steep. Near the end of his life Morihei confessed sadly, "I have given my life to opening this path, but when I look back there is no one following me. . . ." The lamentable lack of harmony among Morihei's disciples and the constant bickering over who is teaching the "real" Aikido are disheartening, and the number of misguided souls—vicious brutes who violate the heart of Aikido by their violence and those who churn up discord with their malicious tongues—encountered during the course of training is distressingly large. The abuses and distortions of Morihei's teaching run on and on.

Still, despite the countless obstacles and setbacks, and the physical and mental barriers, if we train sincerely, centering ourselves between conflicting forces with a pure mind, sooner or later, here or there, the Path that the Founder opened for us will appear amid the raging clouds of darkness and despair and lead us closer to the calm, clear, and harmonious light of Aiki.

Bibliography

The main sources of information on the life of Morihei Ueshiba are as follows.

Kisshomaru Ueshiba (Kodansha). *Aikido kaiso Ueshiba Morihei den* (Founder of Aikido: The Biography of Morihei Ueshiba). This is the "official" biography, published in 1977 by the Founder's son and successor.

Kisshomaru Ueshiba (Kodansha). *Aikido kaiso* (Founder of Aikido). This illustrated biography, full of fascinating photographs taken from all stages of Morihei's career, was published in 1983 on the hundredth anniversary of the Founder's birth.

Kisshomaru Ueshiba (Kodansha). *Aikido shintai* (The Truth of Aikido). Published in 1986, this lavish book contains new information not included in the above two volumes.

Kisshomaru Ueshiba (Kodansha). *Aikido no kokoro* (The Heart of Aikido). An English translation of this work was published by Kodansha International in 1984 as *The Spirit of Aikido*.

Aikido Shimbun (Aikido Newspaper). Published monthly in Japanese by the Aikido Headquarters Dojo, 17-18 Wakamatsu-cho, Shinjuku-ku, Tokyo 162, Japan.

Morihei Ueshiba. *Budo renshu*. First published privately in 1933, this manual was reprinted in 1978 by Minato Research, 20-13, Tadao 3 chome, Machida-shi, Tokyo 194-02, Japan.

Morihei Ueshiba. *Budo*. This manual, published privately in 1938, is currently unavailable to the general public.

Kanemoto Sunadomari. *Bu no shinjin* (True Man of Martial Valor). Tama Publishing Company, Noto-machi 33, Shinjuku-ku, Tokyo 162, Japan. First published in 1969 while Morihei was still living, this biography by the Omoto-kyo believer Sunadomari interprets Morihei's life in light of that religion's teachings.

Hideo Takahashi (ed.). *Takemusu aiki*. Seinen Aikido Doko Kai, Naka-Kokubun 5-26-27, Ichikawa-shi 272, Japan. Published in 1976, this is a collection of Morihei's talks on the spiritual dimensions of Aikido.

Aiki News (in English and Japanese). Demeure Saito, Apt. 201, Daikyo-cho, 3-Banchi Shinjuku-ku, Tokyo 160, Japan. This magazine also makes available films of Morihei.

Aiki Magazine (in Japanese). Takada Baba 1-31-8, Shinjuku-ku, Tokyo 160, Japan.

In addition to the above publications, which largely contain the same material in slightly different versions, I have made extensive use of the vast oral literature that exists, collecting valuable information from public forums and countless private discussions. Much of this was passed on to me with the clear understanding that I would not publicly identify the source—hence the lack of references in the text. In short, this book is a composite of things read, heard, and experienced, one individual's view of Morihei Ueshiba and the art of Aikido. (All of the translations from the Japanese are my own.)

To complete the picture, the reader is directed to my other relevant publications, all published by Shambhala Publications:

Sacred Calligraphy of the East. This book discusses the importance of the role of calligraphy in Oriental thought and life.

The Sword of No-Sword: The Life of the Master Warrior Tesshu. This book discusses the life and teaching of the greatest martial artist of the nineteenth century.

Aikido: The Way of Harmony. Written under the direction of Rinjiro Shirata, this book illustrates the actual techniques of Aikido.

Index

Index